Carol Deacon's
Party Cakes for Children

NEW
HOLLAND

For Kirsty and Emma Davidge who couldn't make it to the shoot
but who have still made it into the book!

First published in 2000 by
New Holland Publishers (UK) Ltd
London • Cape Town • Sydney • Auckland

24 Nutford Place, London W1H 6DQ, United Kingdom
80 McKenzie Street, Cape Town 8001, South Africa
Level 1, Unit 4, 14 Aquatic Drive, Frenchs Forest, NSW 2086, Australia
Unit 1A, 218 Lake Road, Northcote, Auckland, New Zealand

10 9 8 7 6 5 4 3 2 1

ISBN 1 85974 406 0

Editor: Kate Latham
Design: Paul Cooper and Kevin Kilbey
Photographer: Edward Allwright

Editorial Direction: Rosemary Wilkinson

Reproduction by Modern Age Repro House Ltd, Hong Kong
Printed and bound in Malaysia by Times Offset (M) sdn Bhd

ACKNOWLEDGEMENTS:
The author and publishers would like to thank Renshaw Scott Ltd for supplying Regalice (sugarpaste),
Guy, Paul & Co Ltd for supplying vast numbers of cakeboards, Culpitt Ltd for equipment
and Divertimenti for the loan of kitchen utensils featured on pages 26-27.

Carol Deacon would also like to thank Jack and Luke Aldridge-Deacon,
Natalie Allwright, Jemma Blake and Belinda Bellingham for all their help and enthusiasm.
Also a special mention to Joshua Pollins, one of her youngest fans
who will be tickled pink to see his name in print.

To contact Carol Deacon, or for further information on her books, e-mail her at
caroldeacon@hotmail.com or visit her website at www.caroldeacon.com.

Important: In the recipes, use either metric or imperial measurements, but never a combination of the two, as
exact conversions are not always possible. Every effort has been made to present clear and accurate instructions.
Therefore, the author and publishers can accept no liablity for any injury, illness or damage which may
inadvertently be caused to the user whilst following these instructions.

Contents

Introduction

First of all, let me say that this book would never have been put together had it not been for the important little people behind the scenes. I owe a debt of gratitude to my dedicated team of researchers, tasters and testers – Jemma, Belinda, Jack, Luke and Natalie (average age 6). They all worked tirelessly and without complaining (despite the vast amounts of chocolate and gingerbread that they had to consume in the line of duty) to prove that many of the designs in this book are so easy that even a child can make them. Thank you one and all. I hope the chocolate all washed out!

Because I realise that not all people with children are cake decorators by trade, I've tried to make things as foolproof as possible for you. The introduction section answers many of the basic questions about working with sugarpaste which I hope you'll find helpful. Then, with the cakes themselves, I have tried to cover as many children's interests and hobbies as I can, to make that annual dilemma of "What shall I make this year?" that little bit easier. I've given short cuts or alternatives wherever possible and even suggest where it might be best to place the candles on your cake.

Some of the cakes are more of a challenge than others, some are so easy they can be made by a child alone or with a little help from a grown up. But whether you're a child of six or sixty I hope you'll be inspired enough to pick up that rolling pin and get cracking!

Carol Deacon

Introduction to Sugarpaste

Throughout this book I have used one particular icing – sugarpaste. It is so versatile that it can be used to cover cakes and to create decorative models. You can pull it, roll it, stretch it, poke holes in it, colour it and, if in despair, scrunch it up and start again with it. It is so easy to use that even a child can work with it. All of the cakes in this book can be decorated with sugarpaste straight from the packet. You needn't add anything else apart from some colour and a lot of fun.

Here, I have answered the most common questions about working with sugarpaste and I hope that you enjoy making your own creations.

What is sugarpaste?

It's easy for people like me to assume that everyone knows what sugarpaste is. It's basically a mixture of icing sugar, glucose and egg white and is readily available in supermarkets and cake decoration equipment shops. It is also easy to make yourself (see recipe on page 17). The thing that confuses people most is its name, or perhaps I should say names. "Sugarpaste" is the term used in Britain and throughout this book. In the supermarket, you'll find it in the "home baking" section, next to marzipan. It could be lurking under one of its many pseudonyms such as "ready-to-roll icing", "fondant icing", "soft fondant", "rolled fondant", "edible modelling icing", "easy ice" and all sorts of other titles. Don't be daunted, or put off. They are all what we'd term "sugarpaste" and are all basically similar and suitable to use for the designs in this book.

Some brands are available ready-coloured and some are even flavoured. Personally, apart from red and black sugarpaste which take a lot of food colour and physical energy to colour, I prefer to mix my own shades as I find some of the ready-coloured sugarpastes a little too soft for my liking. But, as with anything in life, the best way is to experiment with different brands to see which suits you best.

How do I use sugarpaste?

Keep it covered

There are a few very basic rules that you need to follow when using sugarpaste. The first is to understand that it dries out when exposed to the atmosphere, so you need to keep it covered when not in use.

When you buy it, it will come in blocks ranging from 250 g up to a 20 kg box. As soon as you cut open the packet and pull off the amount you need to use, reseal the packet or tightly wrap in a polythene bag. I buy rolls of small plastic freezer bags from the supermarket which I find ideal for storing all my bits of leftover icing. Then I place the bags into a large airtight plastic box and store it in a cupboard. Different colours should be kept in different bags to stop the colours from bleeding into one another.

Shop-bought sugarpaste has a shelf life of about eight months (check the side of the box as well). Home-made sugarpaste should be used up within a week. Neither type needs to be stored in a fridge.

Dust your surface

When using sugarpaste, always start by dusting your worksurface with icing sugar to prevent it sticking. Keep a small bowl of icing sugar handy all the time to dust your hands, utensils and surfaces. If you're in a humid kitchen or the air is damp, you will be surprised at how sticky your hands can get. Don't worry about any icing sugar smudges on the sugarpaste at this stage, they can be wiped away easily with a damp paintbrush when the cake is finished.

Treat it rough!

Begin by kneading the sugarpaste until it becomes nice and pliable. If it's quite cold in your kitchen then this may mean lots of physical exertion and liberal dustings of icing sugar. If you're trying to soften large quantities to cover a very large cake, break the icing up and knead it in small sections first. Then pile it all up and knead the whole thing together.

Some people prefer to microwave their sugarpaste for a few seconds to soften it but this does have its drawbacks. Apart from the obvious risk of overheating the sugarpaste and possibly causing a nasty burn, microwaving can occasionally cause a skin to form on the surface of the sugarpaste. If it is then used to cover a cake it may crack on the edges and develop a crazy-paving appearance on the top and sides. This won't affect the taste of the icing but will affect your marks if you're planning on entering any cake decorating competitions!

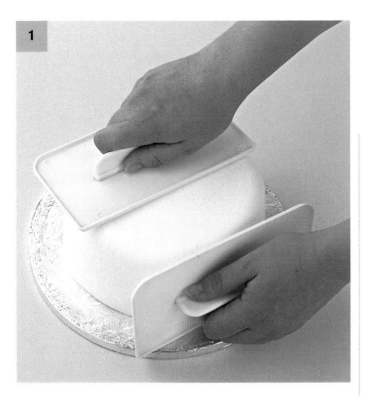

1

Will I need lots of special tools?

Not at all. Most of the equipment used in this book (see page 26), such as rolling pins, knives, drinking straws, paint and pastry brushes you will probably have already, which is why sugarpaste is such an excellent medium for the beginner to use. Where I have used something special such as a cutter, I have tried to suggest alternative methods as well.

If sugarcraft begins to get a grip on you, there are two pieces of equipment that I would recommend you to buy. The first is a turntable which really does make life easier. There are all types – plastic, metal, tilting, non-tilting, raised and flat. It's purely a question of taste and money as to which one you choose – I managed for years with a cheap flat one. You won't need one that tilts unless you're planning on venturing into the highly skilled world of royal icing.

The second piece of equipment that nobody could ever part me from are my cake smoothers (1). These are two pieces of flat plastic with a handle on the back. You hold them as you would an iron and run them over the sides and top of your covered cake to smooth out any lumps and bumps. These little beauties are what will lift your cake's appearance from that of the enthusiastic but probably lumpy-sided amateur to the smooth polished look of the professional. As a temporary measure, you can cut a couple of flat plastic sections out of the top of an ice cream or large margarine carton. They're a little more fiddly to use because you haven't got handles to grip but you can still use them to run around and smooth the top and sides. (See pages 19–20 for instructions on covering cakes and cake boards with sugarpaste.)

Both turntables and smoothers are available from cake decoration equipment shops and you may also find them in some kitchenware shops and department stores.

How do I colour sugarpaste?

The best products to use for colouring your own sugarpaste are food colour pastes. These are of a thicker consistency than liquid colours, so that if you have to use a lot to achieve a dark shade, it shouldn't make the icing too soggy and unmanageable. Most cake decoration shops stock a vast range of colours and you should also be able to find a limited range in the home baking section in some of the larger supermarkets. However, if you can only get hold of liquid colour, don't despair. It is possible to use it but you may have to knead a lot of icing sugar into the icing to stop it from becoming too wet.

2

Apply the paste using the tip of a knife (2) or a cocktail stick. To achieve an unusual shade, you can use more than one colour at a time. If you are creating a new colour, keep a count of how many "dabs" of paste you use and which colours you apply so that you can replicate it later. Then, it's just a question of kneading it in. I am often asked how I get my colours looking so flat and even. The answer is simple – brute force! There is no alternative but to knead and knead and knead until the colour is evenly distributed.

Will the food colour stain?

Most of the colours will wash off your hands extremely easily but for protection against temporary staining from some of the more virulent shades, such as "sky blue" or "mint green", it is worth buying a pack of disposable polythene gloves from the supermarket. A clean pair of washing-up gloves kept especially for this use are an excellent alternative.

Can I mix sugarpaste with sugarpaste?

Yes, you can knead different coloured sugarpastes together to achieve an alternative colour or shade. For example, knead lumps of yellow and pink sugarpastes together to make a flesh colour, or black and white to make grey sugarpaste. If you make a colour that you might want to use again later, keep a note of the colours and rough quantities involved to make it easier to achieve a similar shade.

You can lighten a lump of coloured sugarpaste by kneading some white sugarpaste into it. Similarly, if you're trying to achieve a very dark colour, such as deep red or green, you can knead a little black sugarpaste into it. This will cut down on the amount of food colour you will need to use to create a dark tone. However, this little trick doesn't work with all colours. For example – kneading black sugarpaste into yellow will not give you a deep yellow, only an odd greyish concoction, so experiment with a small piece of sugarpaste first.

Creating special effects

Woodgrain effect

To achieve an easy woodgrain effect, first take a lump of white sugarpaste and a smaller lump of brown sugarpaste. Tear the brown icing into pieces and press it into the white. Roll the two colours together into a sausage, then bend it into a horseshoe shape. Roll the icing into a sausage again, and then fold and roll once more.

Continue until you see a woody effect starting to appear. If you roll the sugarpaste too much and the whole piece turns brown, re-roll some white sugarpaste back into it (3).

Marble effect

Again, this effective look is extremely easy to achieve. Take a lump of white sugarpaste and a smaller piece of the appropriate "vein" colour. In my case, I've used black and white for a white marble effect. Tear the smaller piece of sugarpaste into small pieces and press onto the white sugarpaste.

Carefully roll and knead the two colours together, as above for a woodgrain effect, until a marbled appearance begins to form. If you go too far, reknead a little white icing back into it. In the picture, I have pulled off a small piece and rolled it into a rounded shape for easy and effective pebble and rock shapes with which to decorate your cakes. These rocks also make extremely useful candleholders (4).

Multi-coloured effect

Break three, four or five different coloured lumps of sugarpaste into chunks and lightly press and roll together (beware: if you roll it too much, it will turn into a brown colour). Then roll it out using a rolling pin and a flat, multi-coloured effect will appear (5).

How do I stick the sugarpaste to the cake?

Sponge cakes

The best two "glues" I have found for sticking sugarpaste to the surface of a cake are buttercream (see recipe on page 17) and jam. Personally, I prefer buttercream but obviously it depends on the taste of the recipient. Once you have cut or carved the cake to shape, slice the cake horizontally into two pieces (or more if the cake is deep enough) and fill with buttercream or jam. One layer of each is a nice combination. Reassemble the cake and spread a thin layer of jam or buttercream over the sides and top using a palette knife. As you spread, any gaps or holes in the sponge should automatically be filled, providing a relatively smooth surface for the sugarpaste covering.

If your kitchen is especially hot and humid, you may find it worthwhile to put your buttercreamed cake into the fridge for a couple of hours to "set up". When you take it out again, it will feel like concrete at first but it will be a lot easier to cover as the layers will not be able to "squish" and move around. The refrigerated coated surface will have lost all its adhesive properties temporarily though, so before covering it with sugarpaste, spread another thin layer of buttercream over the top and sides of the cake.

In all of the cake projects, I have used buttercream to stick the sugarpaste to the cake – you can, of course, use jam as a substitute if you prefer.

Fruit cakes

If you are using a fruit cake, you will need to cover the cake with a layer of marzipan before the sugarpaste layer. This is to stop the oils from the fruit cake staining the sugarpaste.

To cover a cake with marzipan, first slice the top of the cake to make it level and turn it upside down on the cake board. If you wish, you can poke a few holes into the cake with a cocktail stick and drizzle a couple of tablespoons of rum or brandy over the top.

The marzipan is stuck to the cake using apricot jam because the taste doesn't interfere with that of the cake. It doesn't matter what brand you use – in fact, often a cheaper jam is better as it contains fewer lumps of fruit. Place a few tablespoons of the jam into a saucepan and heat gently to boiling point. Alternatively, microwave on full power for a couple of minutes until bubbling.

If there is a lot of fruit in your jam, pour it though a sieve to remove the lumps, making sure you press it through with a spoon. Take care as the jam is at boiling point. Then spread the jam over the top and sides of the cake using either a pastry brush or a palette knife. Dust your worksurface with icing sugar (never use cornflour as it can react with the marzipan

and cause fermentation), and roll out the marzipan. Lift and place over the cake. Smooth into position and trim the excess from the base.

To stick the sugarpaste to the marzipan, lightly brush the marzipan with either clear alcohol (such as gin or vodka), boiled water or, if you have some left over, the remaining boiled apricot jam. For instructions on covering cakes and cake boards with sugarpaste, see pages 19-20.

When I'm making models, how do I stick the pieces of sugarpaste together?

I have experimented with all sorts of sugar glues but the easiest, cheapest and least messy solution I have found is plain water. It will work perfectly well for the designs and figures in this book because all of the pieces are stuck together as soon as you make them, so the sugarpaste is still soft, malleable and slightly sticky. For sticking sugarpaste models together, I place cooled, boiled water from the kettle in a small jar kept solely for that purpose. However, if you find something else that works for you, then by all means stick with it (no pun intended).

when you're eating and slice normally. If you're cutting around a template or cutting out a thin, flat shape such as a leaf then hold the knife virtually upright and cut the sugarpaste using the tip of the knife (7).

If you have something very thin and intricate to cut out, then I would suggest using a scalpel with a 10A blade which you can buy from cake decoration and art shops.

How long can I store my sugarpaste models and will the colours fade?

Sugarpaste models can be made up to a month in advance of the date when you need them. Store them in a tin or cardboard box with a lid (never an airtight plastic container) and place in a cool place until required. Don't put them in a fridge or damp garage or they will go soggy. A lid of some sorts is important to protect them from dust and flies and, most important of all, sunlight, because bright daylight will cause the colours to fade.

After their public debut at the party, the birthday person may want to keep the models. The sugar in the icing acts as a preservative and there is nothing in them that will go mouldy, so your models can be kept indefinitely in a box. Out on a shelf, however, the colours will fade and they will become brittle in time and susceptible to moisture. (You can prolong their life slightly by varnishing them using a special varnish available from cake decorating shops.)

The secret for successful and secure "sticking" is not to use too much liquid. If you use too much to stick an ear on the side of a character's head it will simply slide off. Again, if you haven't used enough water it will also fall off, so increase the amount. When you are modelling with sugarpaste, the icing should be pliable and is often fairly sticky. Therefore, it will usually take little more than a light dab of water and a gentle press with the tip of your finger to stick the pieces together, especially the very small elements, such as ears and hands (6).

Very occasionally there will be one element of a design that simply refuses to stay in place and needs sterner measures. The thing that gave me the most trouble in this book was the troll nestling amongst the fir trees on the Christmas cake – for some reason his nose refused to stay where it was put. It was finally fixed in place with a tiny dab of royal icing.

What should I use for cutting sugarpaste?

The best instrument for cutting shapes out of sugarpaste is a small, sharp, non-serrated knife (see Basic Equipment on page 26). When cutting the ends off a sausage shape or cutting out a thick square or rectangle, hold the knife as you would

Troubleshooting

Cracks

Don't despair! This happens to all of us at times. It usually occurs because the sugarpaste has not been kneaded for long enough and therefore is not suitably warm and pliable for use. By far the easiest solution is to hide an offending crack with another model or decoration.

Usually, cracks or creases in chunky shapes, such as sausage or ball shapes, can be got rid of by simply rekneading and reshaping the sugarpaste. If you still have a hairline crack, then gently stroke it away using the pad of your finger. Do think ahead, though, perhaps the shape could be positioned so that the crack is hidden or facing the back of the cake.

Sometimes cracking happens because the sugarpaste is old or has already started to dry out. Microwaving can also cause problems (see page 6). Always cut off any crusty edges from microwaved sugarpaste before using and discard them.

If you have covered your cake with white sugarpaste, and found cracking on the edges, this can usually be hidden by dipping your finger in a little icing sugar and rubbing the sugarpaste gently in a circular motion to fill the cracks. For coloured sugarpastes, take a small lump of the same coloured sugarpaste and polish its base on a shiny surface, then rub the polished surface over the cracks, again using a circular motion.

An alternative method is the plasterer technique. Colour a little royal icing to the same shade as the cake. Spread over the cracks, then carefully scrape away the excess with a knife. This should leave the fractures both filled and hidden.

Watermarks

The secret behind getting rid of watermarks is to deal with them as soon as they occur. If you accidentally splash or drip water onto your cake, wipe it away immediately. If you leave it for too long, the drip will start to dissolve the surface of the sugarpaste and you'll be left with an unsightly hollow. If the sugarpaste is still soft you may be able to smooth out the problem by rubbing gently, in a circular motion, with the tip of your finger. Be careful, though, or you could cause the sugarpaste around the watermark to fracture and crack causing an even bigger problem than before. If all else fails and you're left with an unsightly blemish in an obvious place, resort to the "tried and trusted, never failed yet" technique of placing something over the top!

Air bubbles under the sugarpaste

These occur when air gets trapped underneath the sugarpaste as you cover the cake.

Once you have rolled out and lifted the sugarpaste onto the cake, it is important to start smoothing it into position from the top first. That way, any air on the top of the cake will be expelled out and under the sides before you press these into position.

It is also important to make sure that the buttercream or jam covering the sponge is still tacky. If it has dried out, it won't hold the sugarpaste in position. If some time has passed since you covered your cake, touch and check that it still feels sticky. If it doesn't, spread another thin layer over the cake.

Another tip is not to roll your sugarpaste too thin when covering the cake. A covering less than 5 mm (⅛ in) thick is more prone to air bubbles.

If, despite all your care, you still find an offending lump – resort to more drastic measures. Holding a clean dressmaker's pin or a cocktail stick at an angle, poke a small hole into the bubble and gently press out the air.

Icing sugar marks

These can be removed after the cake is assembled. First of all, gently brush over your masterpiece with a soft brush, such as a pastry brush (use a smaller paintbrush over delicate areas or models). That should remove most of the "dust". For more stubborn areas, wipe away marks using a damp (not wet) paintbrush or a soft, lightly moistened, clean cloth.

Don't worry about how it looks initially, the shiny damp areas will revert to the matt finish of the rest of the cake in a few hours, depending on the temperature and humidity in your room.

Frayed edges when cutting sugarpaste

To cut sugarpaste cleanly, you need a small, sharp, non-serrated knife. A scalpel (available from stationery shops) is also useful for trimming edges and making intricate cuts.

When I turn my cake over to get a nice flat surface on the top, I get a large gap between the base of the cake and the board

If the cake is very rounded, slice away some of the cake before turning it over. If you are using sponge cake and the gap is not too large, simply fill it with buttercream as you coat the outside. If it is too large to do this, roll out a sugarpaste "sausage". Flatten one edge with your finger and slide into the gap (8). Trim away the excess with a sharp knife.

The same procedure is also used on fruitcakes using marzipan instead of sugarpaste.

Basic Recipes

I really believe that it is important for a cake to taste as good as it looks. To help you achieve success in the taste test area, here is a collection of tried and trusted recipes for all the cakes and icings that you might need. There's even a luxurious truffle recipe to help you use up all the leftover bits of cake, because you won't want to throw them away!

Madeira sponge cake

This recipe is probably the quickest, easiest and tastiest sponge cake recipe that you'll ever come across. You simply throw everything in the bowl together, mix and bake. It produces a firm moist cake that is excellent for carving into shapes. It will freeze for up to three months.

Method

1 Grease and line the relevant cake tin and pre-heat the oven to 150°C/300°F/Gas 2.

2 Sift the flour into a mixing bowl and add all the other ingredients. Bind them together carefully using a slow speed setting on your mixer (to stop flour from flying everywhere) then increase the speed and beat for one minute.

3 Spoon the mixture into the prepared tin and smooth the top. Bake in the centre of the oven. Test the cake at the end of the cooking time. If you can hear a lot of bubbling and it still looks very pale leave it in for another quarter of an hour. Test again later by inserting a knife or skewer. If it comes out clean, the cake is cooked. Leave in the tin for five minutes, then turn out onto a wire rack to cool.

Square tin		15 cm (6 in)	18 cm (7 in)	20 cm (8 in)
Round tin	15 cm (6 in)	18 cm (7 in)	20 cm (8 in)	23 cm (9 in)
Self-raising flour	170 g (6 oz)	230 g (8 oz)	285 g (10 oz)	350 g (12 oz)
Caster sugar	115 g (4 oz)	170 g (6 oz)	230 g (8 oz)	285 g (10 oz)
Butter (softened)	115 g (4 oz)	170 g (6 oz)	230 g (8 oz)	285 g (10 oz)
Eggs (medium)	2	3	4	5
Milk	1 tbsp	1½ tbsp	2 tbsp	2 tbsp
Baking time (approx.)	1¼ hrs	1½ – 2 hrs	1¾ – 2 hrs	2 – 2¼ hrs

Taste variations

It's easy to vary the cake's flavour. To add a touch of citrus, mix the grated zest of an orange or lemon to the mixture before cooking. Alternatively a teaspoon of almond essence or 30 g (1 oz) desiccated coconut turns an ordinary Madeira into something quite exotic!

Colour variations

Food colours needn't be limited to use on the outside of the cake. Swirling a little food colour into the mixture before cooking will result in a marbled sponge. Alternatively you could mix it in more thoroughly for a solid coloured sponge.

Fairy cakes

To make the little fairy cakes for the Caterpillar or Horrible Bug cakes, simply mix up the recipe amount required for a 15 cm (6 in) square Madeira sponge cake. Divide into portions and mix a different food colour paste into each portion (apply slowly with a knife). Then spoon into paper cake cases and bake in the middle of the oven (180°C/350°F/Gas 4) for about 15 minutes. This should make about 15 cakes.

Pudding bowl & loaf tin cakes

If you are baking a cake in a 1 litre pudding bowl or 900 g (2 lb) loaf tin for cakes such as the Wicked Witch, Racing Car or Jungle Explorer, again use the recipe amounts for the 15 cm (6 in) square cake.

To prepare a heatproof pudding bowl, grease the inside and place a disc of greaseproof paper or baking parchment at the base of the bowl. When cooked (and because it is so thick, this could take up to 2 hours), slide a knife around the outside of the bowl and tip the cake out onto a rack.

Do the same with the loaf tin. Grease the insides and lay a strip of greaseproof paper along the bottom. Slide a knife down the sides of the cake to loosen after cooking and turn out as before.

Chocolate chip cake

To make a chocolate chip pudding bowl cake, as used for the chocolate Cookie Monster cake or the Rag Doll cake, make up the mixture as for the 15 cm (6 in) square cake as described above and stir in 100 g (3½ oz) chocolate chips. Spoon the mixture into the prepared bowl and bake for the appropriate amount of time.

Chocolate sponge cake

This wonderful recipe produces a cake with a velvety soft texture. Always try to use good strong plain chocolate when making this cake. A crust will form on the top when cooking which may even scorch slightly – this is perfectly normal. All the crust should be cut off and discarded before decorating.

This cake will freeze for up to three months

Method

1 Pre-heat the oven to 180°C/350°F/Gas 4. Grease and line the tin and separate the eggs.
2 Melt the chocolate, either in a small bowl suspended over a pan of simmering water or in a heatproof bowl in the microwave. Do not get any water into the chocolate.
3 Cream the butter and caster sugar together.
4 Beat in the egg yolks and then the melted chocolate.
5 Set the mixer to a slow speed and add the flour. Mix very lightly, just until all the flour is incorporated.
6 Scrape the chocolate mixture into a spare bowl and wash and dry the mixing bowl (you must get rid of any grease).
7 Attach the whisk attachment to your mixer and whisk the egg whites into stiff peaks. Whisk in the sifted icing sugar.
8 Reattach the beater to the mixer and slowly mix the chocolate mixture into the egg whites. Pour into the prepared tin and bake immediately.
9 Because of the crust, it is sometimes difficult to tell if the cake is cooked. If there is a very strong smell of chocolate in your kitchen then that's a good sign. Cut away a piece of crust and insert a knife or skewer. If it comes out clean, the cake should be cooked. Leave in tin for five minutes, then turn out.

Square tin		15 cm (6 in)	18 cm (7 in)	20 cm (8 in)
Round tin	15 cm (6 in)	18 cm (7 in)	20 cm (8 in)	23 cm (9 in)
Eggs (medium)	3	4	6	8
Plain chocolate	150 g (5 oz)	170 g (6 oz)	230 g (8 oz)	285 g (10 oz)
Butter	90 g (3 oz)	120 g (4 oz)	170 g (6 oz)	230 g (8 oz)
Caster sugar	45 g (1 ½ oz)	75 g (2 ½ oz)	120 g (4 oz)	150 g (5 oz)
Self-raising flour	90 g (3 oz)	120 g (4 oz)	170 g (6 oz)	230 g (8 oz)
Icing sugar (sifted)	30 g (1 oz)	30 g (1 oz)	60 g (2 oz)	90 g (3 oz)
Baking time (approx.)	40–55 mins	45 mins –1 hr	1–1¼ hrs	1 – 1½ hrs

Fruit cakes

As well as a recipe for a traditional rich fruit cake oozing with nuts and brandy-soaked fruit, I have also included two non-alcoholic fruit cakes, both of which are slightly sweeter and will perhaps appeal more to children.

Although many people think that making a fruit cake must be a huge binding chore, it's really not. Once you have got all the ingredients together you literally just throw them in, mix them round and bake. You also get the added bonus of being able to make a wish as you stir the mixture and a wonderful aroma floating through your home. You can't buy that at the supermarket!

The amounts given here are for a 20 cm (8 in) round cake suitable for the Christmas cake on page 73. Although not absolutely essential, the rich fruit cake will benefit from being made up to three months in advance and being "fed" every couple of weeks with a little brandy (just drizzle it over the top of the cake and reseal). However, the other two cakes can be made and iced straightaway.

Preparing the tin

Because fruit cakes take so long to cook, it is really worth the effort of double lining the tin to protect the outside of the cake as it cooks. I prefer to use greaseproof paper for this but baking parchment will work just as well.

Rub a little butter or margarine around the inside of the tin to grease it. Cut a sheet of greaseproof paper off the roll long enough to go right around the tin. Cut it in half lengthways to make two long strips. Fold the two strips in half along the length. Place one strip inside the tin to line it and the other around the outside. Tie string round the outside of the tin to hold the external wrapping in place.

Using the baking tin itself as a template, draw around it on another piece of greaseproof paper. Place a second piece underneath the first sheet and cut out two circles of greaseproof paper at the same time, cutting just inside the line. Place these on the base of the tin.

Traditional rich fruit cake

Ingredients
175 g (6 oz / 1 heaped cup) currants
175 g (6 oz / 1 heaped cup) raisins
175 g (6 oz / 1 heaped cup) sultanas
40 g (1 ½ oz / 3 tbsp) mixed peel
75 g (2 ½ oz / ½ cup) glacé cherries (halved)
90 ml (6 tbsp) brandy (for drizzling)
175 g (6 oz / ¾ cup) butter
175 g (6 oz / 1 heaped cup) soft dark brown sugar
4 medium eggs
200 g (7 oz / 1¾ cups) plain flour
1 tsp mixed spice
½ tsp cinnamon
30 g (1 oz) ground almonds
Grated zest of 1 lemon
30 g (1 oz) flaked almonds

Method
1 If you have time, place all the dried fruits into a mixing bowl with the brandy. Stir and cover and leave for a few hours, preferably overnight.
2 Grease and double line the cake tin as described above and pre-heat the oven to 150°C/300°F/Gas 2.
3 Cream the butter and sugar together, then beat in the eggs. Gently stir in the sifted flour, spices and ground almonds (add a little more flour if the mixture is at all runny).
4 Stir in the soaked dried fruits, lemon zest and flaked almonds.
5 Spoon into the prepared tin. Level the top and bake for 2¾ hours. To check whether the cake is ready, insert a skewer or a small sharp, non-serrated knife into the centre. If it comes out clean, the cake is ready. If not, bake for another 15 minutes.

Leave the cake to cool in the tin.

Storing the cake
To store after cooling, pierce the top of the cake a few times with a cocktail stick. Drizzle with a little brandy and double wrap the cake in greaseproof paper. Then double wrap in two sheets of aluminium foil and place in a tin or cool cupboard. Never store in an airtight plastic container. "Feed" by drizzling with a little brandy about once a week. The cake should keep for about three months.

Chocolate fruit cake

This is one of those recipes which at first glance you think couldn't possibly work. Well it does – brilliantly!

Ingredients
175 g (6 oz) butter
175 g (6 oz) brown sugar
4 medium eggs
115 g (4 oz) plain flour
115 g (4 oz) self-raising flour
15 g (½ oz) cocoa
100 g (3½ oz) currants
100 g (3½ oz) raisins
100 g (3½ oz) sultanas
75 g (2½ oz) glacé cherries (halved)
100 g (3½ oz) milk chocolate drops
15 ml (1 tbsp) rum flavouring

Method
1 Line and prepare a 20 cm (8 in) round tin as described above and pre-heat the oven to 150°C/300°F/Gas 2.
2 Cream the butter and sugar together, then beat in the eggs.
3 Sift the flours and cocoa together and stir into the mixture.
4 Stir in the fruit, the chocolate drops and the rum flavouring.
5 Spoon into the prepared tin and bake in the middle of the oven for about 1½ – 2 hours. Leave to cool in the tin before turning out. Store as above.

Tropical fruit cake

The secret ingredient in this little gem of a cake is pineapple. If you wish, you can soak the dried fruit overnight in rum and drizzle a couple of tablespoons over the cooked cake before decorating but it works just as well without alcohol.

Ingredients
200 g (7 oz) self raising flour
½ tsp mixed spice
½ tsp cinnamon
225 g (8 oz) crushed tinned pineapple (well-drained)
150 g (5 oz) butter
125 g (4½ oz) soft brown sugar
2 large eggs
30 ml (2 tbsp) milk
75 g (2 ½ oz) glacé cherries (halved)
120 g (4 oz) sultanas
120 g (4 oz) raisins
120 g (4 oz) currants

Method
1 Line and prepare a 20 cm (8 in) round tin as described above and pre-heat the oven to 170°C/325°F/Gas 3.
2 Sift the flour and spices together into a bowl.
3 Tip the pineapple into the now empty sieve and allow to drain well.
4 Cream the butter and sugar together, then beat in the eggs.
5 Fold in the flour and milk.
6 Roll the cherries in a little flour and add to the mixture. Sir in the fruit and the pineapple.
7 Bake in the centre of the oven for about 1½ hours. Leave to cool in the tin before turning out. Store as above.

Microwave cakes

These may not have exactly the same texture or appearance as the real thing but the advantage is that they only take four minutes to cook. They look a lot paler than a cake cooked in a traditional oven but after they've been covered with lashings of buttercream, they'll disappear in a very traditional manner!

The amounts given are for an 18 cm (7 in) round microwave cake pan or a 1 litre heatproof pudding bowl. Never use a metal cake tin in a microwave.

Microwave vanilla cake

120 g (4 oz) butter
120 g (4 oz) caster sugar
2 large eggs
1 tsp vanilla essence
120 g (4 oz) self-raising flour
½ tsp baking powder

Method

1 Grease and place a greaseproof paper disc on the base of the cake pan or bowl.
2 Cream the butter and sugar together.
3 Beat in the eggs and vanilla essence.
4 Stir in the flour and baking powder.
5 Spoon the mixture into the prepared pan and cook on full power for 4 minutes. Stand for ten minutes before turning out.

Microwave chocolate cake

120 g (4 oz) butter
120 g (4 oz) caster sugar
2 large eggs
30 g (1 oz) cocoa powder
90 g (3 oz) self-raising flour
1 tsp baking powder

Method

1 Follow steps 1-3 as for the vanilla cake above (omitting the vanilla essence in step 3).
2 Stir in the cocoa, flour and baking powder.
3 Cook on full power for four minutes. Leave to stand for ten minutes before turning out.

Gingerbread

90 g (3 oz) butter
150 g (5 oz) soft brown sugar
90 g (3 oz) golden syrup
425 g (15 oz) plain flour
(plus about 30 g/1 oz for
rolling out on)
1 tsp baking powder
2 tsp ground ginger
1 tsp mixed spice
1 medium egg (beaten)
Currants and glacé cherries
(optional)

Method

1 Gently heat the butter, sugar and syrup until the sugar has dissolved. Leave to cool slightly for about five minutes.
2 Pre-heat the oven to 180°C/350°F/Gas 4 and lightly grease a couple of baking trays.
3 Sift the flour, baking powder and spices together into a mixing bowl and make a well in the centre.
4 Tip the melted mixture and the beaten egg into the centre. First bind the mixture together using a knife, then use your hands to form a soft dough.
5 Sprinkle your worksurface with flour and roll out the gingerbread to about 3 mm (⅛ in) thick.
6 Cut out the figures using cutters and trace around the house template (see page 94) using a sharp knife. Re-knead and re-roll the gingerbread as necessary.
7 Lift using a fish slice or palette knife and place onto the baking tray. If you wish to use currants and cherries for eyes, mouth and buttons, gently press these into the gingerbread at this stage. Bake for about 15 minutes in the centre of the oven.
8 Transfer the cooked gingerbread to a cooling rack and decorate in whatever manner you wish when cold.

Chocolate truffles

These are an extremely easy and delicious way of using up leftover bits of cake (vanilla, chocolate or fruit). The trouble is that they are so delicious, you may find yourself having to cook a spare cake especially for the truffles! Boxed up they would make lovely presents.

To make, use approximately 30 g (1 oz) chocolate for every 30 g (1 oz) of cake crumbs.

Melt the chocolate in a heatproof bowl and stir in the crumbs. Roll into ball shapes and either place in tiny paper cases or arrange on a plate. Decorate with melted chocolate and sweets, vermicelli or anything else that you have to hand.

You can use any mixture of chocolate and cake – Madeira cake and white chocolate is a great combination! You can also add a teaspoon of brandy or rum essence if you wish. Decorate with sweets, nuts or yet more chocolate. Experiment and have fun!

Icing Recipes

Buttercream

Buttercream is wonderfully versatile for filling and decorating cakes, as it can be coloured, stippled or piped. This recipe makes up one quantity as referred to in the cake designs. If you have a lot left over, you can freeze it for up to one month

250 g (8 oz) butter
450 g (1 lb) icing sugar
1 tbsp hot water
1 tsp vanilla essence

Method
1 Beat the butter until soft and fluffy.
2 Mix in the sugar, water and essence and beat until soft.

Taste variations

For chocolate buttercream, either mix in 100 g (3½ oz) melted white or plain chocolate or 1 tbsp cocoa powder mixed to a paste with 1–2 tbsp hot water.

For coffee flavouring, mix 1 tbsp instant coffee into 1 tbsp water and beat into the buttercream.

Alternatively you can substitute peppermint, lemon or almond essence in place of vanilla to vary the taste.

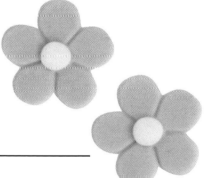

Sugarpaste

Although ready-made sugarpaste is easily available, here is a home-made version that works just as well.

Treat it as you would a commercial brand but use within one week of preparation.

500 g (1 lb 2 oz) icing sugar
1 egg white (or equivalent amount of dried egg white mixed with water)
30 ml (2 tbsp) liquid glucose (available from chemists, supermarkets and cake decorating equipment shops)

Method
1 Place the icing sugar into a bowl and make a well in the centre.
2 Tip the egg white and glucose into the well and stir in using a wooden spoon.
3 Finish binding the icing together with your hands, kneading until all the sugar is incorporated and the icing feels silky and smooth.
4 Double wrap immediately in two small plastic bags. It may be used straightaway.

Royal icing

Traditionally, royal icing is made with real egg white. However, because of the slight possibility of salmonella poisoning, it is better to use dried egg white instead. This works just as well and is easily available from supermarkets or cake decoration equipment shops (it may be called dried egg albumen, "easy egg" or even "meringue powder").

Read the instructions on the packet in case they differ slightly from the ones I've given here.

20 g (¾ oz) dried egg white
90 ml (2½ fl oz) cold water
500 g (1 lb 2 oz) icing sugar

Method

1 Mix the egg white and water in a bowl until smooth.
2 Sieve the icing sugar into a grease-free bowl.
3 Tip in the egg mixture and beat on the slowest speed for five minutes until the icing stands up in peaks.
4 Place the icing into a airtight plastic bowl with a lid. Lay a piece of cling film directly on top of the icing and replace the lid. Always keep covered when not in use.

Royal icing can be stored for up to two weeks in the bottom of the fridge. Allow a couple of hours for it to reach room temperature before use. Beat well before use.

Glace icing

This is a very simple water and sugar icing that is ideal for use on fairy cakes or the top of simple sponge cakes. It can be coloured with a touch of food colour if you wish.

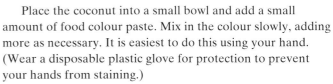

Mix together 120 g (4 oz) icing sugar and 15 ml (1 tbsp) water and spoon over cakes. Allow to set.

Colouring desiccated coconut and sugar granules

This is probably the quickest way of all to cover a cake board. If dessicated coconut is coloured green, it makes realistic looking grass (see Horrible Bug cake on page 40). If coloured grey or brown, it makes marvellous gravel.

Place the coconut into a small bowl and add a small amount of food colour paste. Mix in the colour slowly, adding more as necessary. It is easiest to do this using your hand. (Wear a disposable plastic glove for protection to prevent your hands from staining.)

You can also colour sugar granules in the same way but beware, it does make for a rather crunchy cake!

Basic Techniques

Covering cakes with sugarpaste

Round cakes

To cover a round cake, either shop-bought or home-made, first make sure that your sugarpaste is well-kneaded and pliable. Measure the height and diameter of your cake. Double the height and add this measurement to the diameter, making a note of the total.

Dust your worksurface and rolling pin with icing sugar and roll out the sugarpaste to the size you've just calculated. Don't roll the sugarpaste to any less than 5 mm (⅛ in) thick (if this means that the sugarpaste has to be slightly less wide than your measurement, it shouldn't matter as it will stretch once it is in position).

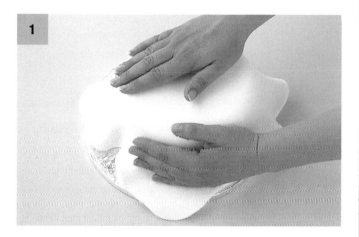

To transfer the sugarpaste from your worksurface onto the cake, you can roll it around your rolling pin and, holding it over the far edge of the cake, pull the rolling pin back towards you allowing the icing to fall and drape over the top of the cake. Alternatively, slide your hands flat, palms upwards under the sugarpaste, and lift and place the icing on top of the cake. If the sugarpaste appears to be sticking to your worksurface, slide a long palette knife underneath it to loosen.

To smooth the rolled sugarpaste into position, start from the top of the cake. Gently stroke the icing away from the centre of the cake to dispel any air trapped between the icing and the cake. Smooth it with the flat of your hand (1) then slide your hands over and around the sides. If the sugarpaste doesn't quite reach the cake board, ease it down by pressing and gently pushing with the side of your hand.

For a final finishing touch, gently rub the heel of your hand over the sugarpaste using a soft, circular motion as though you were gently polishing it. You can also run over the surface with a cake smoother for a really professional touch.

Square cakes

It is just as easy to cover a square cake with sugarpaste as a round cake. The secret is to make sure that you have rolled out the sugarpaste so that it is wide enough to cover the cake comfortably. If you have to pull and stretch the sugarpaste too much it is likely to catch and tear on the corners.

Measure the height, double it and add to the width of your cake. Roll the sugarpaste out to the measurement calculated, and lift and place on top of the cake (as described above). Again, start by smoothing out the icing on the top of the cake using the flat of your hand. Then move on to the sides. Start with a downward stroke with your palm flat against the sides of the cake so that the edge of your hand pushes the icing gently down towards the board. If it starts to form a pleat, hook a finger underneath the icing and pull gently to fan the icing out. Then carefully press the icing into position. Trim away any excess icing from around the base.

The corners and edges on a square or rectangular sugarpasted cake will always be softly rounded so do not spend anxious, frustrating minutes trying to create a razor sharp crease.

Covering cake boards

The all-in-one method

This is by far the easiest and quickest way of covering a board. You do it before the cake is placed onto the board to avoid the need to trim and fit sugarpaste around the cake.

Lightly moisten the cake board with a little water and place it to one side. Knead the sugarpaste until it is pliable and begin to roll it out on your worksurface. Before it has reached the size of the board, lift and place it onto the board. Continue to roll the icing up to and over the edges of the board (2). Smooth it into position with either the flat of your hand or a cake smoother, then trim away the excess and neaten the edges.

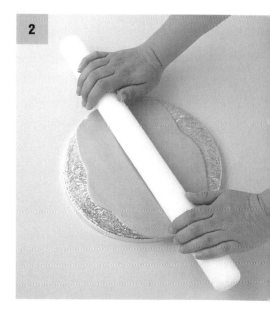

Some people prefer to cut out the icing in the middle, where the cake will eventually sit, at this stage. This is because, after a couple of days, the moisture in the cake will start to dissolve the sugarpaste on the board beneath it. However, in my experience, the cakes are usually eaten so fast that there's little time for any real damage to be done and so far, nobody's ever complained to me about a soggy bottom!

The bandage method

This method of covering the cake board is used after the cake itself is covered and in position on the board. It works best for round, oblong or slightly irregular-shaped cakes.

Run a tape measure around the sides of the cake and make a note of the measurement. Ensure that your worksurface is well dusted with icing sugar and roll some sugarpaste into a thin strip which is slightly longer than the circumference of the cake (as measured) and slightly wider than the exposed cake board (the distance between the side of the cake and the edge of the board). Slice a little icing off one of the long sides of the strip to create a neat edge (the remaining icing should still be slightly wider than the exposed cake board). Moisten the board with a little water. Slide a knife under and along the strip to loosen any sections that might be stuck to the worksurface and roll the sugarpaste up like a loose bandage.

Starting from the back of the cake, slowly unwind the "bandage" over the board so that the cut edge of the strip lies flush against the base of the cake (3). Neaten the join and carefully run the pads of your fingers or a cake smoother over the icing. Trim the edges.

You can also use this method if you're trying to cover a square board around a circular cake.

Covering the board around a square cake

Apart from the all-in-one method, this is the easiest way to cover either a round or square cake board surrounding a square cake.

Roll out the sugarpaste to a thickness of about 3 mm (⅛ in) and cut out four strips slightly longer and slightly wider than the sides of the exposed cake board. Moisten the cake board with a little water and lay one strip along each side so that they overlap at the ends (4). Make a diagonal cut from the edge of the board to the edge of the cake at each corner and remove the excess icing pieces at each corner. You should now be left with a neat mitred join at all four corners. Smooth the icing and run a sharp knife around the edges to trim away the excess.

3

4

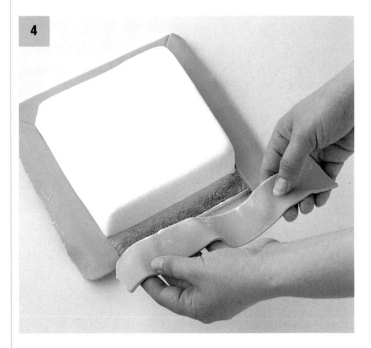

This technique of covering the board in sections also works if you're trying to cover the board around an irregular shape such as the Racing Car on page 78. Moisten the board with water and roll out your sugarpaste. Cut it into sections and lay around the cake until the board is covered. Make a cut across any overlapping icing and lift and remove the excess. Run a knife around the edges to neaten them.

Ribbons on boards

Apart from the Space Age cake (page 30), if you look at any of the main cake photos in the book, you will see that each one is finished off with a ribbon around the edge of the cake board. This little touch is by no means obligatory. It is always done in competitions and displays in the sugarcraft world and it's a habit I just can't seem to kick!

If you'd like to do the same to your cakes, measure the circumference of the board and cut a piece of ribbon to just over that length (allow roughly 10 mm (⅜ in) extra for the overlap). The height of a cake board in this country is usually 12 mm (½ in) but most haberdashers only stock ribbons at widths of 15 mm (⅝ in). Your local cake decorating shop should have a stock of 12 mm width ribbon in various colours.

The best method I have found for keeping the ribbon in place is by using short lengths of double-sided tape. Other methods are non-toxic glue, dressmaking pins or dabs of royal icing. Glue and royal icing may bleed through and discolour the ribbon, and I would never recommend pins on any cake, especially one designed for a child for obvious reasons.

Modelling with sugarpaste

Making figures

If you pull one of the figures in this book apart you will find that in fact it is made out of very simple and easy-to-make shapes. Heads are usually ball shaped, torsos slightly oval and legs are long and sausage-like (5)

When making figures, you have to take into account various factors such as gravity and the strength and ability of the medium itself. Sugarpaste is not ideal for making a three-dimensional ballerina standing on one leg – it simply cannot dry hard or strong enough. That is why you will find that most of the characters in this book are either sitting, lying or using the sides of the cake as support. If your character still seems a little wobbly, then resort to some secret support. Insert a short strand of raw, dried spaghetti or a candy stick (or sweet cigarette as they used to be called). Try to avoid using cocktail sticks as these could cause injury to the unwary eater.

It is because of these various reasons that bed and settee cakes are extremely valuable designs to master. Once you can make a bed, you can put anything or anyone in it from Father Christmas to the family dog!

All the figures in this book are stuck together using water. The secret is not to use too much or bits will fall off! If you haven't already done so, read through the "Introduction to Sugarpaste" section (see pages 6–11) which deals with colouring and using sugarpaste in more detail.

Dressing your characters is the way to really bring them to life. If you are making a cake for somebody who always wears a suit or a certain shirt, dress the character on the cake likewise for added humour. Patterns can be painted on with food colour (6) and small details such as collars or buttons can be cut or rolled out of sugarpaste. Another extremely quick and easy way to make buttons is to press small circles down the front of a character's tummy with the end of a drinking straw.

Making faces

It's amazingly easy to create a variety of different expressions without the need for any artistic skills. Can you draw an exclamation mark? A simple line and dot? Because if so, you can also draw a whole range of different faces.

Over the page are ten drawn examples of very simple faces pulling ten very different expressions and they are all done using just dots and lines (7).

I recommend that you use black food colour and a fine paintbrush to paint the faces onto the sugarpaste. (See "Painting on sugarpaste" on page 24 for further tips.) Alternatively, you could use a food colour pen (a type of felt tip pen that uses food colour instead of ink) which you can buy in cake decorating shops. However, you must allow the sugarpaste to harden for a few hours first otherwise the nib of the pen will rip and tear the surface of the sugarpaste.

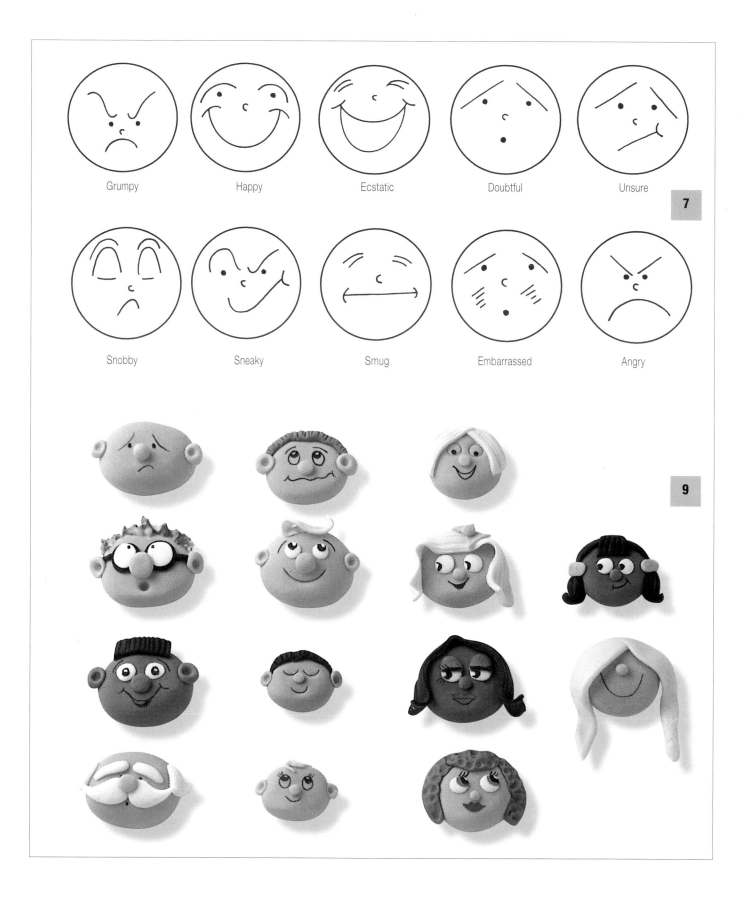

Grumpy   Happy   Ecstatic   Doubtful   Unsure

7

Snobby   Sneaky   Smug   Embarrassed   Angry

9

The beautiful princess face (see page 46) is slightly more difficult but only because you have to try to paint the eyelashes as fine as possible (8). If they're too thick, she'll look like a drag queen!

Alternatively, features such as eyes can be made out of small balls of sugarpaste. Hair can be piped or smeared on using royal icing or buttercream. It can also be cut out of sugarpaste and styled in a multitude of fashions to suit the character of the cake or the recipient (9). You can even press sugarpaste through something such as a sieve or garlic press (washed of course!) to make the most amazing dreadlocks.

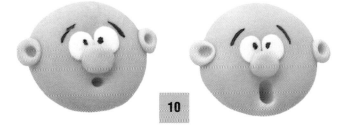

It is useful to note that on most people – ears tend to be level with the eyes. Also, for some reason, my men tend to have bigger noses than my women!

Never underestimate the power of the end of a humble paintbrush! Poke a hollow with it to make an "oh!" expression. Poke and pull it downwards and your character immediately starts singing his heart out (10).

You can also make expressions just by poking curved objects such as icing nozzles or drinking straws into the sugarpaste while it's still soft (11).

When it comes to skin tones, the best colour I have found for white tones is a shade of food colour paste called "paprika", available from cake decoration equipment shops. Alternatively, you can knead a little pink, yellow and white sugarpaste together. For darker skins, use "dark brown" or "chestnut" food colour pastes (11).

Making animals

Many of the same rules apply to making animals out of sugarpaste. Pull a model apart and you'll see that again the basic components are easy-to-make shapes (12). In fact, once you can master the cone, sausage and ball, you can immediately make a teddy, rabbit and baby (13). Baby? Okay so perhaps baby shouldn't come under the animal heading but it's another demonstration of how incredibly versatile these basic shapes can be.

Remember that the finished cake will probably be picked up and moved around. It might even have to travel long distances in a car, so make sure that the models have nice chunky bottoms to sit on, so that they don't fall over and that any appendages – trunks, arms, legs, ears, etc – are stuck down securely, without challenging the laws of gravity.

If you are planning to make a whole cake in the shape of an animal, it might be worth making a small sugarpaste prototype first. This way you can experiment with colours and proportions without fear of too much wastage. You might also come across new ideas to improve the design along the way.

Sugarpaste models can be made at least one month in advance. Store them in a tin or cardboard box for protection (but not an airtight plastic container). Keep somewhere cool, such as a cupboard, but don't store somewhere damp such as the fridge or garage.

Painting on sugarpaste

This is another technique which can look extremely daunting. What if it goes wrong? Will the whole cake be ruined? Again, follow some simple rules and understand the medium and you should be painting masterpieces in no time.

Always use food colour to paint on cakes. You will find a vast range of paste colours in cake decoration equipment shops but you can start with just a few basics and mix them together as you would watercolour paints to get all sorts of colours and shades.

If possible, leave your sugarpasted cake overnight before painting. This means that the surface will have hardened and will be much easier to paint on. You are also less likely to dent the cake if you lean on it.

Brush the surface of the cake with a dry brush to remove any icing sugar which could cause colours to bleed. Place a few dabs of food colour onto a saucer and mix in a little water. You are now ready to start painting.

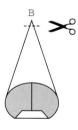

You can paint a very light outline on the cake first or you could follow the tracing technique shown in the Princess cake on page 46 to transfer an image to the top of the cake. If you are planning to draw an outline around the image, paint the colour on first before the black outline to prevent the black food colour from bleeding.

Correcting painted mistakes

To remove a painted mistake, dip a paintbrush into clean water and gently rub the area in a circular motion to break the colour up. Then wipe away with a clean, damp cloth. Leave to dry before repainting.

Piping techniques

Piping is another technique that tends to frighten people, but basic piping techniques are actually quite simple. Practise first on a spare board or worksurface if you don't believe me!

To make life easier, some supermarkets sell ready-made icing in tubes – just screw a nozzle on the end and pipe!

Cake decoration equipment and some kitchenware shops also sell ready-made piping bags but it's not that difficult to make your own.

Making a piping bag

1 Cut some greaseproof (waxed) paper into a triangle.

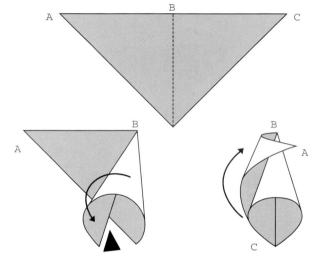

2 Pick up corner "C" and fold over, so that "B" forms a sharp cone in the centre.

3 Wrap corner "A" around the cone.

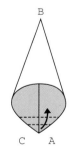

4 Make sure that "A" and "C" are at the back and that the point of the cone is sharp.

5 Fold points "A" and "C" inside the top edge of the bag to hold it securely. Snip off the end and insert a piping nozzle.

Piping

Place some icing into the bag and fold the end over a couple of times to seal it and force the icing down out of the nozzle.

To pipe around the base of a cake or the edge of something such as the decorated background on the Princess cake, a style of piping known as a "snail trail" is often used.

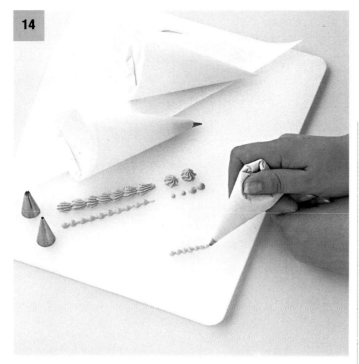

To do this you simply squeeze a little icing out of the nozzle, then keeping the tip of the nozzle inside the icing, release the pressure and pull the bag slightly along the cake. Squeeze the bag again to expel more icing, release and pull (14). Continue along the cake.

By changing the nozzles you get different effects. In the photograph above, you can see the difference between a plain and a star nozzle.

Incorporating candles

Candles are such an important part of a birthday cake that they really need to be thought about right at the beginning of the design stage to make sure that there's room for them. Yet often they are not considered until five minutes before the cake is bought out.

If you make your own candleholders out of sugarpaste then, not only can you be sure that they will fit in with the design, but you can also sit the candles around the board. Make sure both the holders and candles are stuck down safely and securely (you can use a dab of royal icing to be extra sure) and that nothing is overhanging or too close to the flames.

To make rock or pebble holders which are useful for all kinds of cake designs, partially knead a little black and white sugarpaste together to get a marbled effect. Pull off small pieces and roll into chunks. Stick into position and insert a candle in the centre (15).

Small balls of sugarpaste also make ideal candleholders and are easy to make. For something more decorative, roll out some icing about 1 cm (⅜ in) thick and cut out a shape, such as a flower or a star, with a cutter.

Space-fillers

Simple cartoon-style flowers make useful space fillers on cakes and are quick and easy to make. Use a "five petal flower" cutter which you can find at any cake decorating equipment shop. Cut out a flower shape and stick a flattened ball of yellow sugarpaste in the centre (16). Alternatively, you could cut out a series of small discs using something such as a piping nozzle. Arrange them in a circle and again finish off with a yellow sugarpaste centre.

Basic Equipment

RULER

MEASURING SPOONS

SIEVE

MIXING BOWL

Baking tins A good assortment of shapes and sizes is useful.

Board Useful when modelling small sugarpaste items.

Bread knife A long, sharp serrated knife is essential for shaping and slicing cakes.

Cake smoothers By using a smoother like an iron, and running it over the surface of a covered cake, small bumps and lumps can literally be ironed out. Essential for achieving a smooth professional finish (see page 7).

Cocktail sticks These can be used as hidden supports inside models, for adding food colour to sugarpaste, and for making frills and dotty patterns.

Cooling rack Available in all shapes and sizes and used for cooling cakes.

Cutters A vast range is available in both plastic and metal.

Drinking straws These can be used as tiny circle cutters and are ideal for making eyes. Held at an angle and pressed into sugarpaste, they can also be used for making the scales on snakes or dinosaurs.

Greaseproof paper Used for lining tins, making piping bags, storing fruit cakes, and in place of tracing paper.

Measuring spoons A set of standard spoons ensures that you use the same quantities each time you re-make a recipe.

Mixing bowls Even the simplest cake uses more than one bowl, so a good selection of bowls is useful.

Paintbrushes A selection of various sizes is useful. A medium brush is good for sticking things with water when modelling, and a fine brush for adding delicate detail. Although more expensive, sable brushes are the best.

Palette knife (metal spatula) For spreading jam or buttercream, mixing colour into larger quantities of royal icing, and lifting small bits of sugarpaste.

Piping nozzles or tubes A varied selection is always useful and they can always double up as small circle cutters. Metal nozzles are more expensive than plastic but are sharper and more accurate.

Rolling pin A long rolling pin like the one shown will not leave handle dents behind in the sugarpaste. Tiny ones are also available and are handy for rolling out small quantities of sugarpaste when modelling. If you don't possess a small rolling pin, a paintbrush handle will often do the job just as well.

Ruler Not just for measuring, a ruler can also be useful for pressing lines and patterns into sugarpaste.

Scalpel Invaluable when careful cutting is required, such as when scribing around a template.

Scissors A decent pair of sharp scissors is essential for making piping bags, cutting linings for tins, and sometimes sugarpaste.

Sieve (strainer) Vital for sifting flour and icing sugar. Also a useful tool for making bushes or hair by simply pushing a lump of sugarpaste through the mesh.

Small dishes Useful for holding water when modelling, icing sugar when rolling out sugarpaste. Also ideal when mixing food colour into small quantities of royal icing.

Small sharp knife A small kitchen knife with a sharp, straight blade will become one of your most important pieces of equipment.

Soft pastry brush It is useful to have two – one for dampening or cleaning large areas, the other for brushing away dusty fingerprints or specks of dried sugarpaste.

Tape measure Useful for measuring cakes and boards to ensure that you have rolled out enough sugarpaste to go around.

Turntable Although not strictly speaking essential, once you've used one, you'll wonder what you ever did without it. Cheaper versions are available in plastic.

Wooden spoon As well as mixing, the handle can be used as a modelling tool.

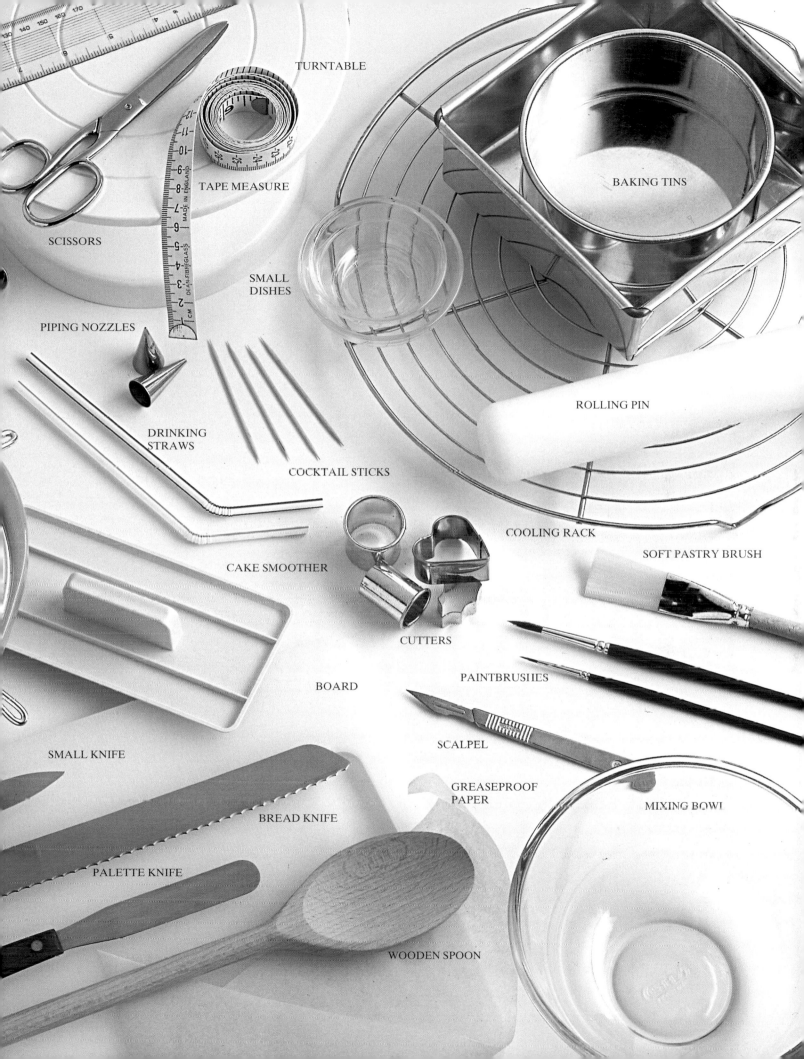

TURNTABLE

TAPE MEASURE

SCISSORS

SMALL DISHES

PIPING NOZZLES

DRINKING STRAWS

COCKTAIL STICKS

BAKING TINS

ROLLING PIN

COOLING RACK

SOFT PASTRY BRUSH

CAKE SMOOTHER

CUTTERS

BOARD

PAINTBRUSHES

SCALPEL

SMALL KNIFE

GREASEPROOF PAPER

MIXING BOWL

BREAD KNIFE

PALETTE KNIFE

WOODEN SPOON

Cakes

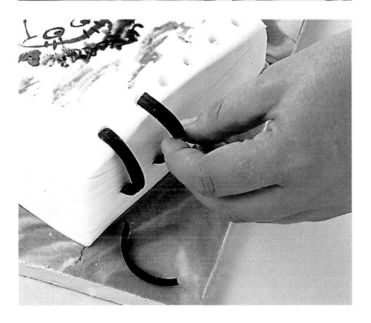

If you have children, then the Horrible Bug cake (page 40), the Upside-down cake (page 58), the Caterpillar cake (page 76), the Gingerbread cake (page 80) and the Cookie Monster cake (page 90) will be of special interest indeed. These are fun cakes, designed especially for children to put together with just a little bit of adult help and guidance.

Although, having said that, when they see how easy sugarpaste is to use, they'll probably want to help make all the rest of the cakes as well!

Space Age

A great cake for any child (or adult) with star gazing tendencies. To give the moon an authentic gravelly look, I covered the cake using marzipan. However, if you don't like marzipan, you could use cream-coloured sugarpaste instead.

1 Carve the edges of the cake into an even dome shape. Slice and fill the cake with buttercream and spread a thin covering around the top and sides. Place two 15 g (½ oz) lumps of white marzipan on top of the cake to form the three-dimensional craters. Knead the rest of the marzipan until pliable. Roll it out and place over the cake. Smooth the surface of the marzipan and trim away any excess from the base of the cake. Place the cake onto the centre of the cake board.

2 Using items with a smooth, rounded end, such as a ball tool or a wooden spoon handle, carefully poke various sized hollows over the surface of the cake to form craters and also make holes in the centre of the two raised craters (1). Try not to break through into the cake beneath. If you do, patch any mistakes with marzipan. Press lines into the sides of the raised craters with the back of a knife.

Use some of the marzipan offcuts to roll moon rocks to place around the top of the cake. (These are also useful for covering any cracks in or blemishes on the marzipan.)

Roll out the dark blue sugarpaste and cover the cake board around the cake using the bandage method of covering (see page 20).

Carol suggests

Don't spread the buttercream too thickly between the layers as there will be a lot of weight on top of the cake and you don't want it breaking through the marzipan.

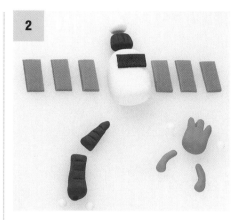

3 To make the green alien (2), first drape two tiny sausage shapes of green sugarpaste over the edge of the rear crater for the alien's arms. Next, roll the remaining green sugarpaste into an oval. Make three cuts in the top and splay slightly.

Stick two tiny discs of white sugarpaste onto the front for his eyes and place the alien's head in the crater.

INGREDIENTS

- 18 cm (7 in) round sponge cake (see page 12)
- 1 quantity buttercream (see page 17)
- 600 g (1 lb 5 oz) white marzipan
- Icing sugar for rolling out
- 150 g (5 oz) dark blue sugarpaste
- 15 g (½ oz) green sugarpaste
- 350 g (12 oz) white sugarpaste
- 30 g (1 oz) red sugarpaste
- Black, edible gold and yellow food colour paste
- 1 strand raw, dried spaghetti (optional)
- 90 g (3 oz) grey sugarpaste
- 30 g (1 oz) black sugarpaste
- 10 g (¼ oz) flesh-coloured sugarpaste

EQUIPMENT

- Carving knife
- Palette knife
- Rolling pin
- Small sharp knife
- 25 cm (10 in) round cake board
- Ball tool or wooden spoon
- Paintbrush

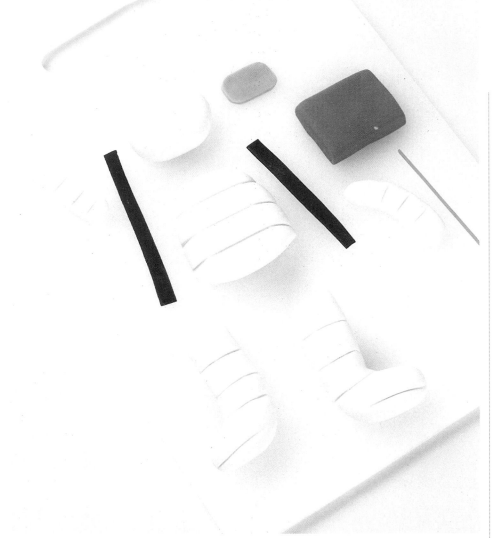

7 Roll 50 g (2 oz) white sugarpaste into an oval for his head and stick onto the body. Roll about 15 g (½ oz) white sugarpaste into a sausage for an arm and stick onto the body. Press lines into the arm as before. Repeat for the other arm. Roll out the flesh-coloured sugarpaste and cut out a rectangle. Cut a tiny triangle off each corner to turn it into an oval shape and stick it onto the front of the spaceman's helmet. Using black food colouring, paint a happy expression on his face.

8 To make the spaceship, roll 60 g (2 oz) of white sugarpaste into a conical shape. Stick a tapering disc of red sugarpaste on top of the cone and top with a small white pointed piece. Press a few lines into the red band. Roll out about 30 g (1 oz) grey sugarpaste and cut out about six small grey rectangles. Place the spaceship into position on the cake and stick the grey rectangles vertically around the ship's base. Stick a small black rectangle onto the front of the ship.

Carol suggests

Instead of painting stars around the cake, you could cut out small sugarpaste star and moon shapes. Alternatively, you could use paper ones – but be sure that nobody eats them!

4 For the worm (2), roll two-thirds of the red sugarpaste into a sausage. Bend one end over slightly to make a head and press a few lines into his back with the back of a knife. Place him into the second crater. Stick two tiny white sugarpaste discs on his face for eyes. Make his mouth by poking the end of a paintbrush into the lower part of his head, pulling downwards slightly. Roll a little more red sugarpaste into a smaller tapering sausage shape and stick this onto the cake as though poking out of a nearby crater. Paint pupils on the eyes of both creatures using black food colour.

5 To make the spaceman (3), roll 90 g (3 oz) white sugarpaste into a conical shape for the body. Press lines back and front with the back of a knife. Stick in position on the cake.

For the legs, take 100 g (3½ oz) white sugarpaste. Cut in two and roll each half into a sausage. Bend one end of each leg up slightly to form a foot and stick the legs into position on the cake. Press lines into the legs as before.

Carol suggests

For extra security for the spaceman's body, stick a strand of raw, dried spaghetti into his torso. Leave a little protruding on which to slot the head.

6 To make the power pack, take 60 g (2 oz) grey coloured sugarpaste and form a rectangle. Stick it on the spaceman's back. Roll out a little black sugarpaste and cut out two thin straps. Stick these across the front of the body.

9 Finally, wipe over the blue border using a damp paint- or pastry brush to remove any icing sugar marks. When it has dried, paint little moons and stars scattered around the base using edible gold or yellow food colour. Highlight the craters by painting them with a little watered-down yellow food colour.

Candles

Make thick sugarpaste or marzipan stars, discs or balls for candleholders, and stick around the outside of the cake board.

Sketchbook

This design should bring out the true artist in you. Don't expect your masterpiece to hang around for too long though, it's far too tasty for that!

1 Begin by slicing a 5 cm (2 in) strip off one side of the cake. Although you won't actually be using this piece, you don't have to throw it away. You could either fill it with a little leftover buttercream to enjoy later with a cup of tea or make it into scrummy chocolate truffles (see recipe on page 17). You should now be left with a rectangle measuring 15 x 20 cm (6 x 8 in).

2 Carefully carve a slight dip out of the middle of the cake (1). If you find this too fiddly, you can leave it flat and level. Slice the cake in half horizontally and fill the centre with buttercream. Reassemble and place the cake slightly diagonally across the cake board. Spread a thin covering of buttercream over the sides and top.

3 Knead 450 g (1 lb) white sugarpaste until pliable. Roll it out and place over the top of the cake. Smooth it into position starting with the top first so that you expel any air that might be

trapped in the "dip". Then move onto the sides. Smooth and trim any excess from around the base.

Before the icing begins to harden, press a few horizontal lines around all four sides of the cake, using either the back of a knife or the edge of a clean ruler, to represent the pages of the sketchbook.

4 To make the very top page of the sketchbook, thinly roll out 200 g (7 oz) white sugarpaste. Cut out a rectangle about 16 x 21 cm (6¼ x 8¼ in) and stick this onto the top of the cake using a little water. Gently tweak back the bottom left-hand corner (2).

Using the end of either a paintbrush or wooden spoon, press a series of shallow holes along the top edge of the sketchbook for the spine binding holes.

5 Paint your picture on your cake with food colours (3) (see page 24 for more information about painting with food colours, and also the variation on page 34).

INGREDIENTS

- 20 cm (8 in) square sponge cake (see page 12)
- ½ quantity buttercream (see page 17)
- Icing sugar for rolling out
- 800 g (1 lb 12 oz) white sugarpaste
- Assorted food colours for painting
- 200 g (7 oz) brown sugarpaste
- 5 liquorice catherine wheels or bootlaces
- 1 tbsp royal icing (optional)
- 20 g (¾ oz) red sugarpaste
- 10 g (¼ oz) grey sugarpaste
- 10 g (¼ oz) black sugarpaste
- 20 g (¾ oz) green sugarpaste

EQUIPMENT

- Carving knife
- 25 cm (10 in) square cake board
- Rolling pin
- Small sharp knife
- Ruler
- Paintbrush
- Cake smoothers (optional)
- Ball tool or wooden spoon

6 To make the woodgrain effect on the board, use 200 g (7 oz) brown sugarpaste and 100 g (3½ oz) white sugarpaste. (See page 8 for details of how to do this.)

Moisten the exposed cake board with a little water and roll out the "woody" sugarpaste. Cut out and cover the board with four triangles. Trim and neaten the edges.

Decorating Variation

You can paint virtually anything you want on top of this particular design. In this example I have gone for something a little more formal which might appeal more to an older child. Alternatively, if painting really isn't your thing, you could write a message instead using a food colour pen (available from cake decorating shops) or just paint or pipe the birthday person's age.

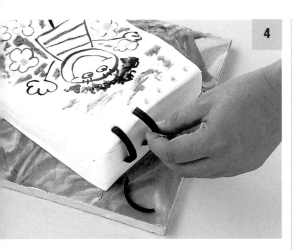

4

7 To make the spiral binding, cut the liquorice into short 7 cm (2¾ in) lengths, one for each hole on the top of the cake. Place a little dab of butter-cream or royal icing into each hole. Make a small slit with the knife about 3 cm (1 in) directly below at the back of the cake. Poke one end of the liquorice into the hole and the other into the slit (4). Apply the rest of the "binding".

For the back of the sketchbook, lay four thin, cut-to-size strips of liquorice around the base of the cake. A little water should hold them in place.

Carol suggests

If you can't get hold of liquorice, substitute thin strips of black sugarpaste or pipe lines of black-coloured buttercream or royal icing instead. Although these methods won't stand proud of the cake, they will still give the impression of spiral binding.

8 To make the paint palette, first roll 40 g (1½ oz) white sugarpaste into a ball. Flatten the ball slightly to make a thick disc and press a shallow hollow into the centre using either a ball tool or the handle of a wooden spoon. Then press a series of smaller hollows in a ring around the central one.

Stick the palette into position on the cake board and fill the hollows with watered-down food colour pastes to represent paints.

9 To make a paintbrush, roll the red sugarpaste into a sausage about 12 cm (5 in) long. Slice a little off one end to neaten it. Roll 5 g (⅛ oz) grey sugarpaste into a small chunky sausage shape and slice a little off both ends.

Press a couple of lines across the top of the grey sugarpaste and stick against the blunt end of the paintbrush handle to form the ferrule. Roll 5 g (⅛ oz) black sugarpaste into a carrot shape and press lines down its length using the back of a knife to look like bristles. Stick in position up against the grey sugarpaste and then lay the paintbrush on top of the cake.

Make a second paintbrush as above using the green sugarpaste for the handle and stick onto the board at the bottom of the cake.

10 To finish off, remove any dusty icing sugar marks from the cake board and liquorice by brushing gently with a damp paintbrush.

Then "splosh" daubs and spatters of food colour around the cake to look like paint marks. (You could leave the board clear, as shown above, to save time.)

Candles

Insert your candles into balls of coloured sugarpaste around the board, set away from the side of the cake. See page 25 for details.

Fairy Town

If there are lots of children coming to the party, you may find that you have to make a few extra toadstools – they look so cute that everyone will want to take one home with them.

1 Begin by carving the cake into a slightly irregular shape by cutting slight slopes and hollows out of it. Then slice the cake horizontally in half and fill with a layer of buttercream. Reassemble and place in the centre of the cake board. Spread a thin layer of buttercream over the outside of the cake. Break and roll 30 g (1 oz) white sugarpaste into four rounded ball shapes. Stick these onto the board around the cake (1).

2 Lightly moisten both the cake board and the positioned sugarpaste balls with a little water. Dust your worksurface with icing sugar and knead 700 g (1 lb 9 oz) white sugarpaste until soft and pliable.

Roll out the icing to a width of about 36 cm (14 in). Lift and place over both the cake and the board. Starting from the top of the cake, smooth and press the icing into position. Trim and neaten the edges.

Carol suggests

Don't panic if for some reason your icing won't cover the entire cake and board in one go. Cover as much as you can and hide gaps, tears or creases with leaves and pebbles later.

3 For the toadstools, take one 45 g (1½ oz) lump and three 30 g (1 oz) lumps of white sugarpaste and mould each piece into a shape like a light bulb (2). Make the base and top of each "light bulb" fairly flat so that they stand securely and support the roof shape.

4 Using a little brown food colour, paint and fill in an arch shape for a front door (see page 24 for tips on painting with food colour). Then paint the outline with black food colour paste. Add a few vertical lines and a dot for the handle. (If you paint the black outline in first, it will simply bleed into the brown.) Still using the black, paint a small arch either side of the door for the windows. Add a small rectangle for the windowsill and a cross for the windowpanes. Repeat on the other toadstools.

5 Stick the toadstool bases on the cake with a little water. Check that they're sitting securely and dab a little water on the top of each one. To make the roofs, divide the red sugarpaste into four pieces. Roll each piece into a flattish disc shape and pinch around the outside edges to thin them. Stick one roof on each toadstool.

Roll tiny little bits of white sugarpaste into minute balls and flatten them to make the spots on the roofs. Stick four or five on each roof.

For the chimneys, roll the black sugarpaste into a thin sausage. Cut off the rounded ends and cut four short, stubby lengths. Stick one on each toadstool roof. Top each chimney base with a tiny triangle rolled out of the leftover black sugarpaste.

Carol suggests

If you are unsure about painting, you could always substitute tiny sugarpaste cut-outs instead for the windows and doors.

INGREDIENTS

- 20 cm (8 in) round sponge cake (see page 12)
- 1 quantity buttercream (see page 17)
- 960 g (2 lb 2 oz) white sugarpaste
- Icing sugar for rolling out
- Brown, black and gooseberry green food colour pastes
- 45 g (1½ oz) red sugarpaste
- 5 g (⅛ oz) black sugarpaste
- 35 g (1⅛ oz) pink sugarpaste
- 5 g (⅛ oz) blue sugarpaste
- 30 g (1 oz) light green sugarpaste
- 30 g (1 oz) dark green sugarpaste
- 10 g (¼ oz) yellow sugarpaste
- 5 g (⅛ oz) flesh-coloured sugarpaste
- 1 tbsp yellow-coloured buttercream or royal icing (see page 18)
- 1 sheet rice paper

EQUIPMENT

- Carving knife
- 25 cm (10 in) round cake board
- Palette knife
- Rolling pin
- Paintbrush
- Small sharp knife
- Pastry brush
- Piping bag (see page 24)
- Scissors

6 Using a large soft brush, such as a pastry brush, dab some watered-down gooseberry green food colour over and around the cake. (Feel free to substitute another shade of green if you don't have gooseberry.)

7 For the pebbles, take two 45 g (1½ oz) lumps of white sugarpaste and 5 g (⅛ oz) pink and 5 g (⅛ oz) blue sugarpaste. Partially knead the pink into one piece of white and the blue into the other to get a marbled effect (see page 8). Pull bits off both pieces and roll into small pebble shapes. Keep about 5–10 g (⅛ – ¼ oz) of each colour for making the fairies' bodies later. Stick the pebbles around the cake and board (3).

8 To make the leaves, thinly roll out both the dark green and the light green sugarpaste. Cut out some very basic leaf shapes (3) using the tip of your knife and stick around the cake using water. (This is an ideal time to cover up any cracks or watermarks on the white sugarpaste.) Scrunch and re-roll the icing as necessary.

9 To make the flowers, use 30 g (1 oz) pink sugarpaste and the yellow sugarpaste. (Instructions for making these are in the Basic Techniques section on page 25.)

10 To make a fairy, first roll either a tiny bit of pale blue or pale pink sugarpaste into a tiny triangle (2). Add a tiny ball of flesh-coloured sugarpaste for the head and tiny sugarpaste marbled strings for the arms and legs. Place the fairies around the cake.

Carol suggests

If a fairy is peeking out from behind a toadstool or from under a leaf, then you don't need to make her legs or wings as they won't be seen.

11 Paint two tiny black dots on each face for the fairy's eyes and place a tablespoon of yellow coloured butter-cream or royal icing into a piping bag (see page 24 for instructions on making a piping bag). Snip a tiny triangle off the end of the bag and pipe an abundance of squiggly hair onto each fairy.

Finally, for the fairies' wings, cut some tiny heart shapes out of a sheet of rice paper. Bend each heart in half and press onto a fairy's back. As it dries, the hair should hold it in place.

Candles

Stick your candles into the icing pebbles around the cake. Be sure to keep them away from the fairies' wings and any overhanging toadstool roofs.

Baby Dinosaur

Aah, this little guy looks almost too cute to eat and is very easy to make. If you want to incorporate candles into the design, do read the note at the end before you start making the cake.

1 If your cake rose a little too enthusiastically in the oven, you may need to take a slice away from the top so that it will sit comfortably and squarely upside-down on the cake board. Next, slice the cake horizontally a couple of times and sandwich the layers back together again with buttercream. Spread a thin covering of buttercream over the top and sides.

Roll out and cover the cake with the duck egg blue sugarpaste. Smooth the icing and trim around the base of the cake. Keep any excess and roll into little eggs for decorating the board or for use as candleholders.

2 Divide and roll about 30 g (1 oz) of both pale yellow and pink sugarpaste into small egg shapes.

3 Mix some blue food colour paste into some water. With a large soft brush, such as a pastry brush, flick and splatter the cake and the little eggs with the coloured water using light, controlled movements (1).

4 To make the baby dinosaur itself, begin with the head. Take 60 g (2 oz) pale yellow sugarpaste and roll into a thick sausage shape. Bend one end forwards to form the head. Press a dent using your finger across the head to make the dinosaur's forehead and ease the mouth area into a slightly pointed shape (2).

5 Stick two flattened ovals of white sugarpaste onto the head for his eyes. Paint the pupils, eyelashes and a mouth using black food colour.

6 Stick the head in position on top of the egg using a little water. Decorate the head and neck with a few scales made by pressing the edge of a drinking straw held at an angle into the icing to leave small "U" shape imprints.

7 Paint some cracks around the dinosaur using a little black food colour. Don't worry if your hands are shaky – jagged, sudden movements will only make the cracks more authentic (3).

8 To make the arms, divide 10 g (¼ oz) pale yellow sugarpaste in half. Roll into two small sausage shapes. Squash and flatten one end of each sausage to make the hands and press a couple of lines into each hand using the back of a knife. Bend and stick the arms into position with a little water.

9 Use 30 g (1 oz) pale yellow sugarpaste for the tail. Roll it into a tapering sausage shape and stick onto the cake board. Paint a few cracks in the shell around the tail.

10 Moisten the exposed cake board and place the smaller eggs around the base of the cake. Carefully spoon the light brown sugar onto the board between the eggs.

Candles

If you want to use candles it would be better to use a larger board. Alternatively, position the cake towards the back of the board and insert your candles into the small eggs at the front.

INGREDIENTS

- 1 pudding bowl cake (see page 13)
- ½ quantity buttercream (see page 17)
- Icing sugar for rolling out
- 400 g (14 oz) duck egg blue sugarpaste*
- 150 g (5¼ oz) pale yellow sugarpaste
- 30 g (1 oz) pale pink sugarpaste
- Blue and black food colour pastes
- 5 g (⅛ oz) white sugarpaste
- 45 g (1½ oz) light brown sugar

EQUIPMENT

- Carving knife
- Palette knife
- 20 cm (8 in) round cake board
- Rolling pin
- Small sharp knife
- Pastry brush
- Paintbrush
- Drinking straw

NOTE: Make duck egg blue sugarpaste by mixing a little green (mint green) and blue (blueberry) food colour pastes into white sugarpaste. Or, you might be able to find a paste called "eucalyptus" which is ideal.

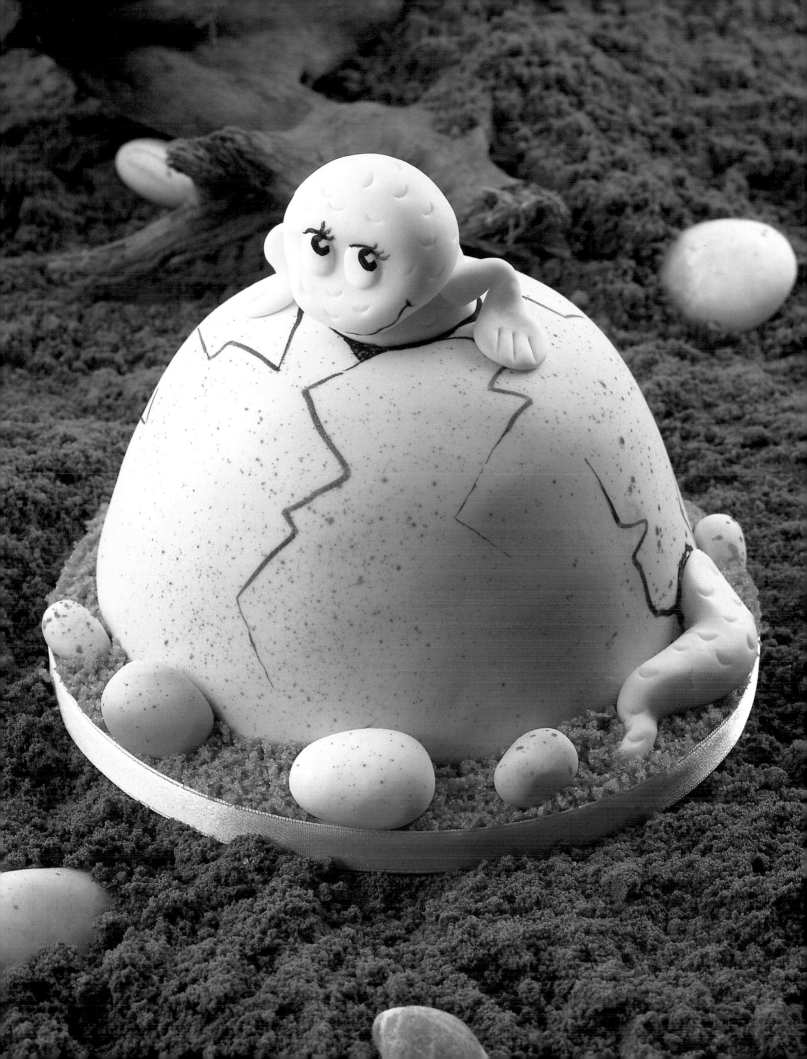

Horrible Bug

The base for this cake needn't involve any baking at all. I used a ready-bought Swiss roll and mini rolls for speed and because it meant my helpers and I could eat any leftovers!

The fairy cakes are so easy to do that it's worth making a whole batch of mini green bug and ladybird cakes, so everyone at the party can have one.

1 Make up a batch of fairy cake mixture as described on page 13. Before you spoon it into the paper cases, divide in two and stir some green food colour paste into one half and red food colour paste into the other. Bake and allow to cool.

2 Place the Swiss roll on the cake board. Cut a small amount of cake diagonally off one end of the mini roll and place up against the Swiss roll so that it pokes out at an angle. Roll out the white marzipan. Cut out two discs and stick on the ends of the branches with buttercream. Paint a few age rings on the discs with dark brown food colour paste. Spread the chocolate buttercream over the log (1) then "rough it up" using a fork to give it a bark-like effect.

Carol suggests

Of course, you can bake a cake if you want to. Simply cut about a third off a square cake. Place the thinner rectangle at an angle to the thicker one to form the branch shape and round all the edges slightly.

3 To make a snail, roll the grey sugarpaste into a slightly tapering sausage, about 18 cm (7 in) long. Starting from the thin end, roll about half of the sugarpaste into a coil. Bend

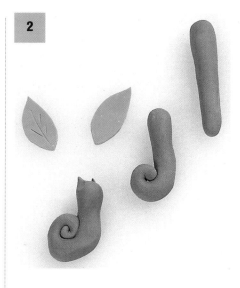

the head forward slightly and pinch two feelers into the top. Add black food colour dots for his eyes and a curvy line for his smile (2).

INGREDIENTS

- Batch of fairy cake mixture (see page 13)
- Green, red, dark brown and black food colour pastes
- Swiss roll (plain or chocolate)
- Mini roll (plain or chocolate)
- 30 g (1 oz) white marzipan
- 2 quantities chocolate buttercream (see page 17)
- 30 g (1 oz) grey sugarpaste
- 30 g (1 oz) red sugarpaste (per ladybird)
- 15 g (½ oz) black sugarpaste (per ladybird)
- 15 g (½ oz) white sugarpaste
- Liquorice bootlace
- 2 long jelly snake sweets (or sugarpaste snakes, see page 84)
- 30 g (1 oz) green-coloured desiccated coconut
- 50 g (2 oz) green sugarpaste

EQUIPMENT

- 30 cm (12 in) round cake board
- Carving knife
- Rolling pin
- Paintbrush
- Palette knife
- Fork
- Small sharp knife

Decorating Variation

Here is a version made by two little helpers – Jemma and Belinda – a very splendid variation indeed. Search out jelly creatures at your local sweet shop to make this an extremely quick-to-make cake. Alternatively, have fun creating your own horrible bugs to decorate the log.

4 To make a ladybird, take a red fairy cake, peel off the paper case and turn upside-down. Spread a little buttercream around the outside of the cake. Roll out about 30 g (1 oz) red sugarpaste for each ladybird and use to cover. Stick a flat, black sugarpaste semi-circle towards the front of the body and paint a black line down the centre of its back. Stick four small flattened black sugarpaste discs onto the back. Make the eyes out of white sugarpaste and stick onto the black semi-circle with buttercream. Paint the pupils with black food colour. Insert six short lengths of liquorice into the body to make the legs.

Carol suggests

If you don't want to paint eyes, you can make them out of sweets such as milk and white chocolate buttons.

5 To make a green bug, take a green-coloured fairy cake, peel off the paper case and turn it upside-down. Add eyes and legs as for the ladybird in the previous step (3).

6 Place the insects, snail and jelly snakes into position on and around the log. Moisten the cake board with a little water and spoon the coconut around the log. Finally, roll out the green sugarpaste and cut out some very simple leaf shapes (2). Press a few veins into the leaves using the back of a knife and arrange and position on the cake.

Candles

Insert the candles into thick sugarpaste discs or balls and stick around the outside edge of the board, well away from the cake.

Football Team

Here we have the entire football team arranged as though posing for a photograph. You could personalize the colours to match those of your favourite team. Although the front row have complete bodies, those behind are only heads and torsos. If you run out of members, fill the gaps with referees, coaches or even team mascots.

1 First prepare the cake. Lay it on its side and cut right through the middle of the cake diagonally. Turn the smaller section upside-down and lay on top of the other (1). The two stacked cakes should now form a triangle. Shave away irregular pieces of cake to make them nice and smooth. Carefully slice both cakes in half horizontally and fill with buttercream. Reassemble and "glue" the two cakes together with more buttercream. Place the cake into position on the centre of the cake board and spread a thin layer of buttercream over the top and sides.

Carol suggests

Buttercream the sides first. This allows you to hold the cake steady by the top and should stop your fingers from getting too sticky.

2 Knead 500 g (1 lb 2 oz) black sugarpaste until pliable. Roll it out and lift and place over the cake. Starting from the top, smooth the icing into position then neaten the base of the cake. Don't worry about icing sugar marks – they will be dealt with later.

3 Moisten the cake board around the base of the cake with a little water. Knead and roll out 250 g (9 oz) white sugarpaste and cover the board using four strips (see page 20 for instructions on this method).

4 When making the footballers, begin with the top row. For each body use 45–60 g (1½–2 oz) white sugarpaste. Substitute a different colour if necessary depending on the team you're depicting. Roll each body into a conical shape, with a flat top to rest the head on. Stick four torsos in a line across the top of the cake. For extra security, insert a short length of raw, dried spaghetti into the top of each body leaving about 1.5 cm (⅝ in) protruding. Roll about 15 g (½ oz) flesh-coloured sugarpaste into a ball for a head. Dab a little water onto the top of the body and slot the head into position. Add heads to the rest of the bodies along the row (2).

5 Make eight small white triangles for the collars. Again, leave these out or alter the colour depending upon the team. Paint the features on the faces and the stripes on the shirt (see pages 21–24 for hints about painting faces and painting on sugarpaste).

It's easier to paint the faces at this stage rather than when the cake is assembled or you might lean on the ones in front and squash them!

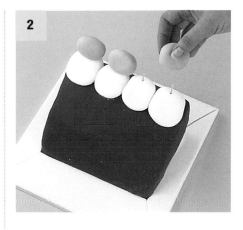

6 Give all the top row some hair. To do this, cut strips out of sugarpaste, press lines down its length and lay over the top of the head. Alternatively you can cut tiny fringe shapes or pipe or dab on squiggles of buttercream or royal icing. Add tiny sugarpaste balls for noses and ears.

Carol suggests

Buy packs of ready-to-use coloured writing icings which are ideal for making "quick hair".

INGREDIENTS

- 20 cm (8 in) square cake (see page 12)
- 1 quantity buttercream (see page 17)
- Icing sugar for rolling out
- 600 g (1 lb 5 oz) black sugarpaste
- 1100 g (2 lb 8 oz) white sugarpaste
- 5 strands raw, dried spaghetti
- 250 g (8 oz) flesh-coloured sugarpaste
- Black, blue and gooseberry green food colour pastes
- 60 g (2 oz) brown sugarpaste
- 10 g (¼ oz) yellow sugarpaste

EQUIPMENT

- Carving knife
- Palette knife
- 25 cm (10 in) square cake board
- Rolling pin
- Small sharp knife
- Paintbrush

Decorating Variation

The nice thing about this design is that it could be adapted for virtually any sport – netball, cricket or even a whole class of schoolmates! In this variation, depicting a basketball team, the characters are made larger than the footballers in order to fill the space.

3

7 Stick a second line of bodies and heads below the first and fill any gaps between the characters with arms. To make each arm, roll about 5 g (⅛ oz) white sugarpaste into a sausage shape. Bend a little at the elbow and stick into position. Add an arm to both of the end characters on the top row.

Flatten a small ball of flesh-coloured sugarpaste for each hand and stick on the end of each arm. Paint the features and stripes onto the characters on the second row with the food colour pastes. Add hair as before.

8 To make the front row, begin with the feet. Roll eight 5 g (⅛ oz) bits of black sugarpaste into ball shapes. Slightly flatten one end of each boot and stick them onto the board, a little in front of the cake with the most bulbous part pointing forwards. For each pair of socks, use 5 g (⅛ oz) white sugarpaste and divide in half. Roll into two chunky disc shapes (3) and press a couple of creases across the top of each with the back of a knife. Stick one on each boot.

9 For each pair of legs, roll 10 g (¼ oz) flesh-coloured sugarpaste into a sausage about 7.5 cm (3 in) long. Cut it in half and stick as though protruding from the top of the socks. Use the cake itself to provide support. For each pair of shorts, roll and shape 10 g (¼ oz) white sugarpaste into a rectangle. Partially cut through the centre of the rectangle and splay slightly. Butt up and stick against the top of the legs and onto the cake.

10 Add the bodies and heads as before. Stick a 15 g (½ oz) white ball of sugarpaste on one of the laps and paint a pattern on it with black food colour paste. Add arms and hands to the front row and the end characters on the second row. Paint in the features, stripes and add hair.

Carol suggests

Position and stick the scarves strategically to hide any imperfections, cracks or lumps in the icing on the sides of the cake.

11 To make the dangling scarves on the ends of the rows, roll out about 30 g (1 oz) white sugarpaste and cut out four thin strips about 6–8 cm (2¼–3 in) long. Fringe one end of each strip and drape one over the outside arm of the footballers on the second and top rows. Paint on the stripes in the appropriate team colour.

Finally dab some watered-down gooseberry green food colour around the base of the cake and brush away any icing sugar marks on the black sugarpaste with a damp paintbrush.

Candles

In order to incorporate candles into this design, you should be able to stand candles in icing "pebble" candleholders (see page 24 for instructions) on the board to the sides of the cake. With very little extra work, you could also make some more footballs to stand the candles in. Keep well away from the overhanging scarves though!

Princess

What little princess wouldn't love a cake like this? Add wings and a wand and you have a fairy princess. Alternatively, dress the princess in white and add a groom and you have a novel wedding cake.

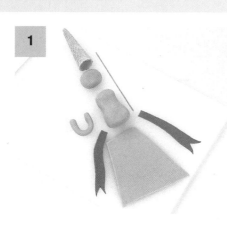

1 Moisten the round cake board with a little water. Cover it with 200 g (7 oz) white sugarpaste (see page 19). Place the board to one side to allow time for the sugarpaste to harden.

2 Carve the sponge into a slightly irregular shape. Slice the cake horizontally and fill with buttercream. Reassemble and place onto the square board, making sure that there's at least a 2 cm (¾ in) gap between the cake and the back of the board. Spread a thin layer of buttercream over the sides and top of the cake and moisten the board.

3 Knead and roll out 700 g (1 lb 9 oz) white sugarpaste to a 36 cm (14 in) square. Lift and place over the top of the cake allowing it to fall over the cake board as well. Starting from the top of the cake, to try and prevent air from getting trapped, smooth the icing into position over both the cake and the board. Trim and neaten the edges.

4 To make the princess, begin with her body. First, roll 60 g (2 oz) pink sugarpaste into a conical shape (1). Stick into position about 4 cm (1⅝ in) back from the front of the cake.

To give added support, you could poke a length of raw, dried spaghetti down the centre of the body leaving about 2.5 cm (1 in) protruding on which to slot her head.

5 Roll out 75 g (2½ oz) pink sugarpaste for her skirt and cut out a tapering rectangular shape (1). Place the shape flat on your worksurface. Place a paintbrush handle on top and roll the brush backwards and forwards along the skirt to frill it slightly (2). Stick the skirt against the front of the body, allowing it to fall down the front of the cake.

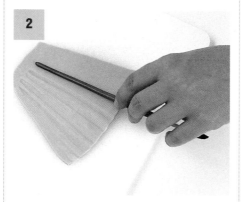

6 Next, roll 15 g (½ oz) flesh-coloured sugarpaste into a ball for her head. Paint in her features (see template on page 23) with black food colour. Stick the head into position on top of the body, taking care not to squeeze the sides of the head and distort her face.

7 Roll 5 g (⅛ oz) flesh-coloured sugarpaste into a small banana shape for her arms and stick on the front of the body. Roll out 15 g (½ oz) mauve sugarpaste and cut out two thin strips about 10 cm (4 in) long. Cut a triangle out of one end of each strip and stick onto the front of her skirt.

8 To make the roses for the bouquet, take a tiny bit of mauve or white sugarpaste and press it between your fingers and thumb to flatten it into a small, thin strip. (You might need to dip your fingers in icing sugar first to stop it from sticking.) Roll the strip up like a loose bandage and tweak the top edges out slightly (3). Stick onto the front of the bodice with a little water.

Make about ten white and five mauve roses to form a bouquet shape.

INGREDIENTS

- Icing sugar for rolling out
- 1 kg (2 lb 4 oz) white sugarpaste
- 20 cm (8 in) square sponge cake (see page 12)
- 1 quantity buttercream (see page 17)
- 150 g (5 oz) pink sugarpaste
- 2 strands raw, dried spaghetti
- 30 g (1 oz) flesh-coloured sugarpaste*
- Assorted food colours for painting the background, including black, yellow, and green
- 30 g (1 oz) mauve-coloured sugarpaste*
- Ice cream cone
- 1 quantity royal icing (see page 18)
- 15 g (½ oz) green sugarpaste
- 5 g (⅛ oz) yellow sugarpaste
- 60 g (2 oz) pale pink sugarpaste

EQUIPMENT

- 25 cm (10 in) round thin cake board
- Rolling pin
- Serrated carving knife
- 25 cm (10 in) square cake board
- Palette knife
- Paintbrush
- Small, sharp knife
- 3 piping bags (see page 24)
- Greaseproof or tracing paper
- Non-toxic HB pencil
- Saucer or paint palette
- Star piping nozzle

*NOTE: To create a mauve-coloured sugarpaste, use "grape violet" food colour paste and for a flesh tone, use "paprika" food colour paste.

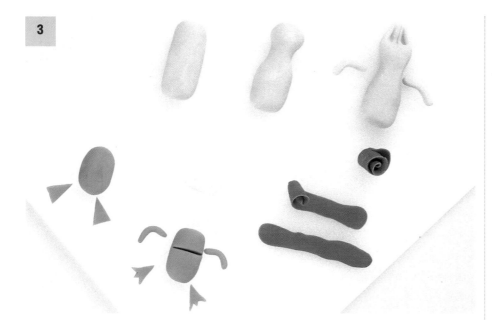

9 To make her hat, cut the end off an ice cream cone. To do this it is best to use a serrated knife and to cut it using a light sawing motion all the way around the cone. Gently press the cone onto the top of her head. (If you press too hard, her expression will turn very ugly indeed.)

10 Place about two tablespoons of yellow-coloured royal icing into a piping bag. Snip a small triangle off the end and pipe hair all around the base of the cone and down onto her

skirts and cake. There's no real professional term for this technique, just allow it to fall into wiggles and squiggles as you go (4).

11 To make the veil on the hat, roll out 15 g (½ oz) white sugarpaste and cut out a thin, tapering strip about 18 cm (7 in) long. Press a couple of lines down its length with the back of a knife. Dab a little water on the top of the cone and wind and drape the strip around her hat. Wedge it securely in amongst her hair at the base.

12 For the frog, roll 10 g (¼ oz) green sugarpaste into an oval shape. Press a line into the top of the oval for his mouth (3). Cut out two tiny green triangles for his feet and cut little "V" shapes out of the end of them to give a webbed-foot appearance. Stand and stick the oval on top of the feet. Add two tiny strings of green sugarpaste for his arms and two tiny balls of white sugarpaste for his eyes.

Cut out a small yellow serrated shape for his crown and stick behind the eyes. Paint two black food colour dots onto the eyes and stick the frog at the princess' feet.

13 To make each rabbit, roll about 20 g (¾ oz) pale pink sugarpaste into an oval shape. Squeeze it slightly, just below one end to form a sort of skittle shape (3). Pinch the top of the head into a point for his ears. Make a cut from the tip of the ears to the top of the head to divide the ears and press the end of a paintbrush into each one to give them some form. Tweak into position. Give both rabbits a ball of white sugarpaste for a tail and add two tiny strings of pink sugarpaste to each for their paws. Paint dots on the face for the eyes and nose and stick into position on the cake.

14 Fill any gaps around the front and sides of the cake with additional coloured roses and balls of white sugarpaste. Place a little green-coloured royal icing into a piping bag and pipe leaves amongst the flowers. These are not complex to do – just pipe a dot then pull the bag away to leave a small tail.

15 To decorate the background, first trace the drawing on page 93 onto tracing or greaseproof paper using a non-toxic HB pencil. Then, turn the paper upside-down and re-trace over the outline on the other side of the paper. Carefully stand the background cake board on the base cake board, against the back of the cake, and draw a soft line to show where it comes up to. Your illustration must not fall below this line or it will not be seen. Lay the covered cake board back on your worksurface and place the drawing (right way up) on top of it. Carefully trace over the outline for a third time (5). You should now have transferred the image onto the cake board.

Carol suggests

Hide any tears, cracks or exposed cake board with rounded balls of white sugarpaste.

Decorating Variation

You could paint whatever you want on the background or if you find painting too difficult, use sugarpaste cut outs instead. On this variation, the board was covered with pale blue sugarpaste and decorated with a simple cut out sun and cloud design.

16 Paint the colour onto the design first before the outline otherwise the black food colour paste will simply bleed into the colour. (See page 24 for hints and tips about painting on

5

sugarpaste.) If you're right-handed, begin painting on the left-hand side so that you don't smudge the food colour as you work. If you're left-handed, start from the right-hand side.

Paint lightly up to the pencil outline. Leave to dry and then paint in the black food colour outlines.

17 When the painted cake board is dry, "glue" the painted background to the back of the cake with dabs of royal icing

When finished, place a plain or star nozzle into a piping bag (see page 24 for instructions on making a piping bag). Fill with about 3 tablespoons of white royal icing and pipe a "snail trail" around the edges of the background board (6). (See page 24 for instructions.) If you find this too tricky, leave the edge plain or pipe a line of simple dots instead.

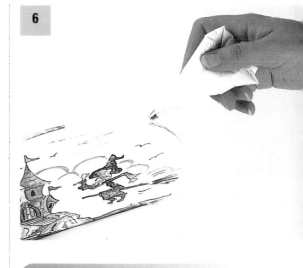

6

Candles

Insert candles into balls of white sugarpaste and stick on top of the cake in the space behind the princess. (See page 25 for instructions.)

Sleepy Puppy

To make the golden brown colour for the puppy, either knead some orange or brown sugarpaste together or colour some white sugarpaste using "autumn leaf" food colour paste. Alternatively, you might be able to buy a ready-coloured sugarpaste called "teddy bear brown" from your local cake decorating shop. Or you could make him a different colour completely!

1 Moisten the cake board with a little water and cover using the pale blue sugarpaste (see page 19 for details.) Place the covered board to one side.

2 Level the top of the cake if it's very rounded. Slice horizontally and fill with buttercream. Reassemble the cake and spread a thin covering of buttercream over the top and sides. Cover and keep the leftover buttercream. Lift up the cake using a fish slice so you don't get your fingers all sticky and place it slightly towards the rear of the board.

3 For the dog basket, roll 100 g (3½ oz) dark brown sugarpaste into a sausage about 50 cm (20 in) long. Cut into four equal lengths and stick them on top of each other on the right hand side of the cake (1).

Press diagonal lines going in alternative directions into each of the strands. Repeat with another four strands on the other side of the cake.

4 To make the puppy's slipper, roll two 60 g (2 oz) lumps of red sugarpaste into flat, chunky oval shapes and cut one in half. Scrunch up one of the halves and stick on one end of the other oval (2). Place the remaining half over the top of the scrunched oval to form the foot of the slipper.

Using either a section of a jam tart cutter or a large drinking straw, cut a "bite" out of the heel. Stick the slipper slightly towards the left of the front of the cake.

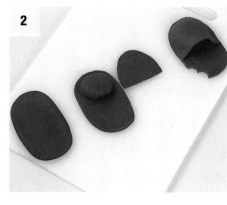

5 To make the puppy's head, roll 200 g (7 oz) golden brown sugarpaste into a thick oval. Flatten one end slightly to form the dog's forehead (3). Bend this thinner end up at a right angle and stick against the cake allowing the muzzle to rest on the cake board.

Press a short vertical line into the front of the dog's face using the back of a knife to make his mouth and poke three small hollows into his muzzle with the end of a paintbrush.

6 Roll two 30 g (1 oz) pieces of golden brown sugarpaste into tapering carrot shapes then flatten them slightly to make his paws. Stick one resting possessively on the slipper (most of this will be hidden by his ear later) and the other just touching his muzzle. Press three lines into the end of each paw with the back of a knife.

INGREDIENTS

- Icing sugar for rolling out
- 300 g (10 oz) pale blue sugarpaste
- 18 cm (7 in) round sponge cake (see page 12)
- 1 quantity buttercream (see page 17)
- 250 g (9 oz) dark brown sugarpaste
- 150 g (5 oz) red sugarpaste
- 350 g (12 oz) golden brown sugarpaste
- 550 g (1 lb 3 oz) white sugarpaste
- 30 g (1 oz) black sugarpaste
- Black and brown food colour pastes
- 15 g (½ oz) yellow sugarpaste
- 15 g (½ oz) green sugarpaste
- 15 g (½ oz) dark blue sugarpaste

EQUIPMENT

- 30 cm (12 in) round cake board
- Rolling pin
- Carving knife
- Palette knife
- Fish slice (optional)
- Small sharp knife
- Jam tart cutter or drinking straw
- Paintbrush
- Fork

7 For the eyes, cut two small round discs out of about 15 g (½ oz) white sugarpaste and pull them slightly to form ovals. Stick them onto the dog's face. Add two smaller black ovals for the pupils and two tiny white sugarpaste dots for highlights.

Roll 10 g (¼ oz) golden brown sugarpaste into a ball and flatten into a disc. Cut the disc in half to make his eyelids. Stick one half over each eye at an angle.

8 To make his nose, roll about 5 g (⅛ oz) black sugarpaste into an oval. Stick onto the muzzle and top with a tiny round, white sugarpaste highlight.

For the ears, make two 30 g (1 oz) golden brown sugarpaste ovals. Flatten the two ovals slightly and stick against the head allowing them to flop over the eyes and paws. Colour the remaining buttercream brown and carefully spread onto the ears. "Rough up" the buttercream with a fork to give them a hairy effect.

Carol suggests

You can leave the ears plain if you prefer or if you want to save a bit of time.

9 Stick two 20 g (¾ oz) lumps of white sugarpaste on top of the cake to form the bumps under the blanket and moisten them with a little water.

To make the blanket, roll out 450 g (1 lb) white sugarpaste to about 15 cm (6 in) square. Break and roll about 15 g (½ oz) each of yellow, green, red and dark blue sugarpaste into small balls and place onto the white. Continue to roll out the icing to about 23 cm (9 in) square, pressing the coloured balls into the white as you go (4). Slice a little off all four edges to neaten them. Cut a fringe into two opposite sides. Carefully lay the blanket so that it covers all the exposed cake but leaves the dogs face and some of the wicker basket showing.

10 To make the dog biscuits, make two 15 g (½ oz) dark brown sugarpaste sausages and press and flatten both ends of each sausage. Using the end of a paintbrush, push the icing in slightly at either end of the biscuit to form a bone shape. Press a line of dots down the centre of the bone with the end of a paintbrush and stick them on the board around the puppy.

To finish, paint a few lines on the slipper with black food colour.

Candles

Insert the candles into thick sugarpaste discs or balls and stick around the outside edge of the board, away from the sides of the cake.

Fishing Pond

To save time on party day, you can make this cake, up to the end of step 6, three days before the cake is required. However, don't place the sugar water into position onto the cake more than one day before, or the moisture from inside the cake will make it dissolve.

1 Slice away the top of the cake to make it nice and level and split the cake once in half horizontally. The height of the cake should be no more than 6 cm (2¼ in). Place the cake onto the board. Fill the centre with buttercream and spread a thin covering over the top and sides.

2 Knead 400 g (14 oz) white sugarpaste until pliable. Roll it out and cover the cake. Smooth the icing into position. Trim and keep the excess from around the base of the cake. Moisten the exposed cake board with a little water. Roll out the leftover white sugarpaste and cover the board (see the bandage method, page 20). If you don't seem to have any leftover sugarpaste, use an extra 120 g (4 oz).

3 Lightly moisten the top of the cake with a little water. Knead and roll out 120 g (4 oz) blue sugarpaste. Cut out a 20 cm (8 in) round disc using either a cake board, plate or your baking tin as a template.
   Lay on top of the cake and paint a light line of water around the outer edge of the disc. Roll 120 g (4 oz) of blue sugarpaste into a long, even sausage about 60 cm (24 in) long. Lay around the edge of the disc to form a large donut shape (1).

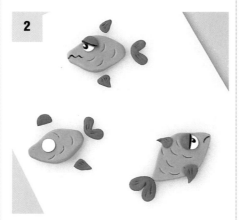

4 To make the fish, take one 20 g (¾ oz) lump and two 15 g (½ oz) lumps of orange sugarpaste. Roll, flatten and shape each piece into a flattish lemon shape for their bodies (2). (They must lie lower than the height of the disc around the edge of the pond, so don't make them too fat.) Stick a flat white disc onto each fish for eyes.

5 Knead about 10 g (¼ oz) red sugarpaste into 20 g (¾ oz) orange sugarpaste. Use this orangey-red sugarpaste to make triangular fins, semi-circular eyelids and tails. Stick these onto the fish. Press a couple of lines into the fins and tails using the back of a knife and a few scales onto the fishes' bodies using the edge of something circular such as a piping nozzle or a lid.

Paint in the eyeballs, mouths and eyelashes with some black food colour and a paintbrush.

6 Place the fish into position inside the pond. Fill the gaps with a few small white flattened sugarpaste "air bubbles". Divide and roll about 10 g (¼ oz) green sugarpaste into four or five thin strands and lay amongst the fish to look like reeds. Place the cake to one side to allow time for the fish to dry out.

INGREDIENTS

- 20 cm (8 in) round sponge cake (see page 12)
- 1 quantity buttercream (see page 17)
- 650 g (1 lb 6 oz) white sugarpaste
- Icing sugar for rolling out
- 250 g (9 oz) blue sugarpaste
- 75 g (2½ oz) orange sugarpaste
- 15 g (½ oz) red sugarpaste
- Black and green food colour pastes
- 45 g (1 ½ oz) green sugarpaste
- 15 ml (1 tbsp) sunflower oil
- 30 g (1 oz) black sugarpaste
- 75 g (2½ oz) golden brown sugarpaste *
- 15–20 clear boiled sweets

EQUIPMENT

- Carving knife
- 25 cm (10 in) round cake board
- Palette knife
- Rolling pin
- Small sharp knife
- Paintbrush
- Piping nozzle or small lid
- 18 cm (7 in) round metal baking tin
- Aluminium foil
- Wire rack
- Pastry brush
- Heart cutter (optional)

* NOTE: To make golden brown sugarpaste, either use "autumn leaf" food colour paste or a ready-coloured sugarpaste called "teddy bear brown". Alternatively, you could knead a little orange and white sugarpaste into some brown sugarpaste.

7 To make the water for the pond, pre-heat your oven to 200°C/400°F/Gas 6. Line the round metal baking tin with aluminium foil and brush lightly with a little oil. Unwrap and place 15–20 clear boiled sweets into the tin and place into the oven for 10–15 minutes until the sweets are bubbling and have melted and covered the base of the tin. Remove the tin from the oven and leave to cool. When cooled (only about 20 minutes), carefully peel off the foil and transfer the circular sugar water disc to a wire rack until needed (3).

8 Holding the "water" by its edges, lift and place on top of the pond (4). To make the rocks, partially knead together about 200 g (7 oz) white sugarpaste and the black sugarpaste for a marbled effect (see page 8 for instructions). Pull off small pieces and stick around the top and bottom edge of the pond to cover all the ragged edges.

Carol suggests

Don't worry about air bubbles in or ragged edges on your sugar water. Bubbles will actually add to the authenticity of the water and the edges will be hidden later.

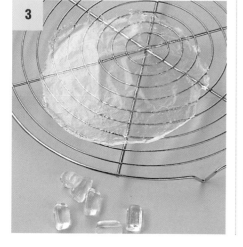

9 Splodge a little watered-down green food colour paste around the sides and base of the cake using a soft brush such as a pastry brush.

Make the lily leaves by thinly rolling out about 30 g (1 oz) green sugarpaste, and cutting out six heart shapes using a cutter or the tip of your knife. Press a few veins onto each one using the back of your knife and place on top of the "water".

Reserve a tiny bit of green sugarpaste for making the cat's eyes later and roll the remaining green sugarpaste into thin strings for the lily leaf stems.

10 To make the cat's paws, first roll two 5 g (⅛ oz) pieces of golden brown sugarpaste into small tapering sausage shapes. Make a couple of small cuts in the end of each one for his claws (5). Stick the paws into position; one slightly bent on the edge of the pond, the other reaching across as if to catch a fish.

11 To make the cat's head, roll and mould 60 g (2 oz) brown sugarpaste into a flattish conical shape. Roll 5 g (⅛ oz) white sugarpaste into an oval for his muzzle. Flatten and bend it slightly and stick onto the lower part of his face.

Roll together a tiny piece of white sugarpaste and a tiny bit of green sugarpaste and make two flat, light green lemon shapes for his eyes. Stick these onto his head at a slight angle. Roll a tiny bit of brown sugarpaste into two "S" shapes for his eyebrows and stick them over the eyes.

Carol suggests

When cutting the cake, remove the "water" first to prevent it shattering.

Carol suggests

As long as you don't make it too tall, the head should sit quite securely on it's own. However, if you're worried about it falling off, insert a strand of raw, dried spaghetti into the edge of the cake and slot the head on top.

12 Make two tiny brown sugarpaste triangles for his ears and stick onto his head. Paint the pupils on the eyes, and the mouth and whiskers on the muzzle. (Don't add the stripes yet on the sides of his head or you'll get it all over your fingers when you stick it onto the cake.) Roll a tiny piece of red sugarpaste into a very small piece of white sugarpaste to make a pink dot for his nose and stick a tiny red sausage on his mouth for his tongue. Stick the head into position on top of the arms. Paint a couple of black stripes on the paws and also on the top and sides of the head.

Candles

It should be possible for you to insert your candles gently into the rocks around the top edge of the pond.

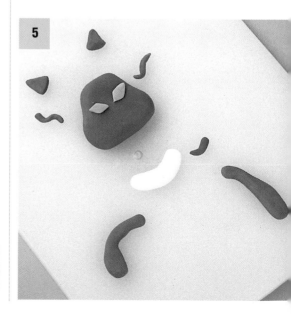

Doll

Make your cake designs sit up and take notice with the aid of two pudding bowl cakes. As a tasty alternative to sponge, you could substitute the chocolate chip cakes as used in the Cookie Monster cake on page 90 instead.

1 Take the two cakes and slice a little off the base of one cake so that it sits comfortably on the board and won't fall over. Turn the second cake onto its side and slice away a strip of cake from the base so that it sits securely on top of the first cake (1).

If the top of the base cake is too rounded and the head falls off, slice a little off the top of the first cake to flatten it. Carve away any unsightly corners on the second cake to make a rounded head shape. Remove the head cake and place to one side.

2 Slice and fill the base cake horizontally with one or two layers of buttercream. Don't overdo it though – the body will have to support a lot of weight and if you sandwich it using too much buttercream, it will simply squish out of the sides of the cake. If you are using a chocolate chip cake as a base then you won't need to fill with buttercream – it should be rich enough without a filling. Place the base cake towards the rear of the cake board.

3 Spread a thin layer of buttercream over the outside of the cake. Knead and roll out 400 g (14 oz) of pink sugarpaste. Place over the cake and smooth into position. Trim away any excess from around the base and place the cake and board to one side. Buttercream and cover the head with 300 g (10½ oz) flesh-coloured sugarpaste. Trim and neaten the icing around the base.

4 For added security to stop the head from falling off the body, you could push a plastic cake dowel through the middle of the base cake. It should go right down until it reaches the cake board, leaving about 5–8 cm (2–3 in) protruding from the top. Place the head into position (2).

5 For the eyes, roll out 30 g (1 oz) white sugarpaste and cut out two discs using a circle cutter or lid. Pull each of the circles to stretch it into an oval shape and stick onto the face. Stick a small ball of flesh-coloured sugarpaste underneath for her nose.

Paint her eyeballs, eyelashes and mouth using black food colour and a paintbrush (see page 24 for hints about painting on sugarpaste). Also paint a few freckles around her nose and two discs on her cheeks with red food colour paste.

Carol suggests

Remember that you can use decorative features, such as the collar and mobcap, to hide any problem areas.

INGREDIENTS

- 2 pudding bowl cakes (see page 13)
- 1 quantity buttercream (see page 17)
- Icing sugar for rolling out
- 450 g (1 lb) pink sugarpaste
- 450 g (1 lb) flesh-coloured sugarpaste*
- 560 g (1 lb 4 oz) white sugarpaste
- Black and red food colour pastes
- 300 g (10½ oz) pale blue sugarpaste
- 200 g (7 oz) yellow sugarpaste

EQUIPMENT

- Carving knife
- Palette knife
- 25 cm (10 in) square cake board
- Rolling pin
- Small sharp knife
- Cake smoothers (optional)
- Plastic cake dowel (available from cake decorating shops)
- Assorted circle cutters or lids
- Paintbrush

* NOTE: To make flesh-coloured sugarpaste, use either "paprika" food colour paste or a mixture of yellow and pink sugarpastes.

1

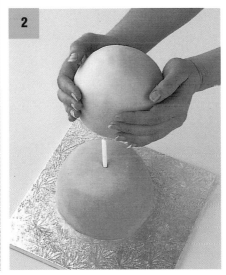

2

Decorating Variation

He may look totally different to the doll but, essentially, this cheeky soccer player is constructed in exactly the same way. Dress him in your favourite team's colours. Follow the instructions up to step 6 (except you'll probably need to make the shirt a different colour – you don't see many soccer players in pink!) (Also, leave out the eyelashes.) Instead of a skirt, use four short stubby sausages of white sugarpaste for the shorts and the socks and two flesh-coloured sausage shapes for the legs. Add a football and a couple of discs of flesh-coloured sugarpaste for his ears.

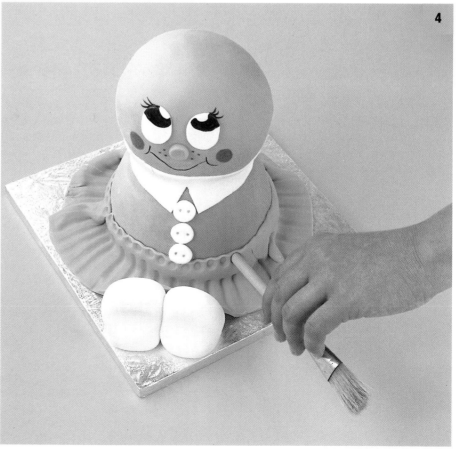

6 To make the collar, thinly roll out 60 g (2 oz) white sugarpaste and cut out a strip about 3 x 15 cm (1 x 6 in). Make a partial cut through the centre and lay the collar around the doll's neck. The cut should automatically part at the front of the doll to form a collar (3).

7 To make the buttons, roll and squash three 5 g (⅛ oz) balls of white sugarpaste into three flattish discs. Stick them down the centre of the doll and press a couple of hollows into each button with the end of a paintbrush. Make two 100 g (3 ½ oz) ovals for her feet and stick onto the board (4).

8 For the skirt, roll out 250 g (9 oz) pale blue sugarpaste. Cut out a large horseshoe shape. Press a paintbrush along the length of the skirt (see the Princess cake on page 46 for a picture of how to do this) then wrap and stick the skirt around the base of the doll. The join should be at the back. Don't worry if it doesn't meet at the back as it won't be seen. Using the end of a paintbrush, poke a line of small hollows around the waistband to neaten it (4).

9 Make two 60 g (2 oz) flesh-coloured sugarpaste sausage shapes for the arms and stick into position on the body.

Roll 30 g (1 oz) pink sugarpaste into a ball for the sleeves. Flatten into a disc and cut in half. Stick one half over the top of each arm (5).

10 To make the hair, first roll out 120 g (4 oz) yellow sugarpaste and cut out a 15 cm (6 in) disc. Press lines across the circle using the back of a knife and cut in half (6). Stick in position on the front of the head. To make the plaits, divide 45 g (1½ oz) yellow sugarpaste in half and roll each half into a sausage. Flatten one end of each and cut a fringe. Press diagonal lines down both plaits and stick onto the head.

11 For the bows, cut two rectangles out of 15 g (½ oz) blue sugar-paste. Squeeze the centre of each rectangle and stick a small rectangle across it. Press a few lines either side of the centre and stick onto the plait.

12 To finish, roll out 250 g (8 oz) white sugarpaste and cut out a disc about 23 cm (9 in) in diameter for the mobcap. You can either do this free-hand or use a plate or cake board as a template. Frill around three-quarters of the outside of the disc by rolling a paintbrush backwards and forwards. Moisten the top of the doll's head and stick into position.

Candles

There should be enough room at the sides of the board to stick some candles inserted into thick sugarpaste discs (see page 25 for instructions).

Upside Down

You get two cakes for the price of one with this design. Can you see the two faces? No. . . only one? Then turn your book upside down and look at the picture again.

Now can you see it?

If you are planning to use candles on this cake, please read the note at the end first.

1 If your cake rose in the oven to give you a nice domed top, enhance it by shaving off any irregularities and any particularly crusty bits to give it an even, rounded finish. If your cake decided to go for a flatter effect in the oven, simply cut away the crust and round the edges slightly.

2 Slice and fill the middle of the cake with buttercream. Reassemble the cake and place in the centre of the cake board. Knead and roll out the flesh-coloured sugarpaste and place on the cake. Smooth out the top and sides and trim. Keep the excess from around the base for making the ears and nose later.

3 To make the hair/beard, break up and place the milk chocolate into a heatproof bowl. Either place in a micro-wave and cook on full for 1–2 minutes until all the chocolate has melted (the time will alter depending on the power of your machine) or, alternatively, place a little water in the base of a saucepan and rest the bowl on top of the sauce-pan. (The base of the bowl should not be touching the water.) Allow the water to simmer gently until the chocolate has melted. Stir as necessary. Be careful not to get any water inside the bowl or the chocolate will turn gritty.

4 Carefully stir the breakfast cereal into the melted chocolate (1). Add a little more cereal if it looks too runny. Then carefully spoon it onto the cake (2). The chocolate cereal should go around roughly three-quarters of the cake and be especially thick on the top of the head/bottom of the face part.

Don't worry if it all seems to be falling off the cake. As the chocolate starts to set, it will "glue" the cereal together and keep itself in place on the head.

5 When you have arranged the hair/beard around the face to your satisfaction, you can add the face. Take 10 g (¼ oz) leftover flesh-coloured sugarpaste, roll it into a ball for the nose and flatten it slightly into a disc shape. Stick in position in the centre of the cake, just below/above the line of hair/beard.

INGREDIENTS

- 18 cm (7 in) round sponge cake
- 1 quantity buttercream (see page 17)
- Icing sugar for rolling out
- 400 g (14 oz) flesh-coloured sugarpaste*
- 100 g (3½ oz) milk chocolate
- 30 g (1 oz) rice-based breakfast cereal
- 20 g (¾ oz) white sugarpaste
- Black food colour paste

EQUIPMENT

- Carving knife
- 20 cm (8 in) round cake board
- Rolling pin
- Cake smoothers (optional)
- Small sharp knife
- Heatproof bowl
- Spoon
- Paintbrush
- 2 m (79 in) ribbon
- Scissors
- Clear sticky tape

NOTE: To make the flesh-coloured sugarpaste you can either colour white sugarpaste with a food colour paste called "Paprika" available from cake decorating shops. Alternatively you can knead a little pink-coloured sugarpaste or food colour paste into a piece of yellow sugarpaste.

3

To make the eyes, take two 10 g (¼ oz) lumps of white sugarpaste, roll them into balls and then flatten slightly into two thick discs. Stick one on either side of the nose (3).

6 Take a 20 g (¾ oz) piece of flesh-coloured sugarpaste and divide it into two pieces for the ears. Roll each piece into an oval shape and stick them to the side of the cake, level with the nose and eyes. Using black food colour paste, paint pupils onto the eyes and then add two slightly curved lines for the mouth/forehead

(See page 24 for notes about painting on sugarpaste if you are worried about making mistakes.)

Carol suggests

The ears should be long and thin rather than rounded, or else gravity will make them fall off the cake.

7 Finally, cut a length of ribbon about 70 cm (28 in) long. (If you have used a larger cake, measure the circumference first with a tape measure as you will need this length plus extra for the bow.) Wrap around the sides of the cake and secure the join with clear sticky tape. The join should be at the top of the head/bottom of beard where it will be hidden by the bow. Tie the remaining ribbon into a bow and trim the ends if necessary. Stick in position using a little melted chocolate or buttercream.

Candles

As the cake takes up virtually all of the board, you will have to use a larger board (25 cm (10 in) diameter minimum) if you wish to add candles.

Position the cake off-centre on the larger board so that the bow sits on the very edge of the board well away from the candles which should be set at the opposite end in sugarpaste holders (see page 25).

Cheeky Pets

I thought this cake might strike a chord with many pet owners. Certainly, "Twiggy", my German Shepherd, is up on the sofa as soon as my back is turned! The wonderful shaggy dog here is piped using royal icing. However, if you prefer your dogs less crunchy, you can use buttercream instead. Beat your buttercream on high for about five minutes and you'll find that it eventually turns white!

1 Begin by covering the cake board. Partially knead 300 g (10 oz) white and 60 g (2 oz) dark brown sugarpaste together to achieve a woodgrain effect (see page 8). Moisten the entire cake board with a little water and cover it using the "all in one" method (see page 19). Trim and neaten the edges and press lines into the icing to give the effect of floorboards using the edge of a ruler or the back of a knife. Place the covered board to one side.

2 To shape the cake, first of all, cut it in half horizontally. Then slice about 2.5 cm (1 in) lengthways off one of the strips and place to one side (1). Place the smaller of the two remaining pieces on top of the larger piece, in an upright position, to form the back of the sofa, slicing a little off it if it is too thick.

Cut two small rectangles out of the remaining thin slice of cake for the arms. Stick them into position and then round the edges of the arms and back slightly.

3 Carefully dismantle the cake. Slice the base horizontally and fill with a layer of buttercream. Reassemble and "glue" the back and arms into position with a little buttercream, then place into position on the covered cake board. Carefully spread a thin covering of buttercream over the outside of the cake.

Carol suggests

Buttercream the top edge of the sofa last. This allows you to hold the cake steady while you buttercream the rest without getting too sticky.

4 For the throw, knead the terracotta-coloured sugarpaste until pliable. Roll it out and cut out a rectangle at least 40 x 30 cm (16 x 12 in).

Press diagonal lines in both directions across the sugarpaste (2) and cut a fringe around the edge. Carefully lift and, moving from the front, drape it casually over the cake. Don't worry if it tears in the seat area – any problems here will be hidden by the dog! Poke dots into alternate squares of the throw with the tip of a cocktail stick.

INGREDIENTS

▸ Icing sugar for rolling out
▸ 500 g (1 lb 2 oz) white sugarpaste
▸ 60 g (2 oz) dark brown sugarpaste
▸ 20 cm (8 in) square sponge cake (see page 12)
▸ 1 quantity buttercream (see page 17)
▸ 650 g (1 lb 7 oz) terracotta-coloured sugarpaste *
▸ 100 g (3½ oz) green sugarpaste
▸ 60 g (2 oz) blue sugarpaste
▸ 5 g (⅛ oz) black sugarpaste
▸ 5 g (⅛ oz) pink sugarpaste
▸ 45 g (1 ½ oz) grey sugarpaste
▸ 3 tbsp white royal icing (see page 18)
▸ 1 tbsp grey-coloured royal icing
▸ Black food colour paste

EQUIPMENT

▸ 30 cm (12 in) round cake board
▸ Rolling pin
▸ Small sharp knife
▸ Ruler
▸ Carving knife
▸ Palette knife
▸ Cocktail stick
▸ Large drinking straw
▸ 2 piping bags (see page 24)
▸ Scissors
▸ Paintbrush

* NOTE: to make terracotta-coloured sugarpaste you can either use a shade of food colour paste called "paprika" which you can find in cake decorating shops or through mail order (see Suppliers on page 95). Alternatively, knead 600 g (1 lb 5 oz) orange sugarpaste and 50 g (1¾ oz) dark brown sugarpaste together.

5 To make the cushions, cut two flattish squares out of the green sugarpaste. Tweak the corners and place into position on the sofa. To form the buttons on the cushions, press four tiny circles into each cushion using the end of a large drinking straw.

6 To make the rug, take 50 g (1¾ oz) blue sugarpaste and roll it out to a 5 mm (⅛ in) thickness. Lay about 5 thin strips of white sugarpaste on the top and roll over them with a rolling pin (3). Cut the sugarpaste into a rectangle and fringe the two ends. Lay and stick the rug in front of the sofa in a slightly crumpled position.

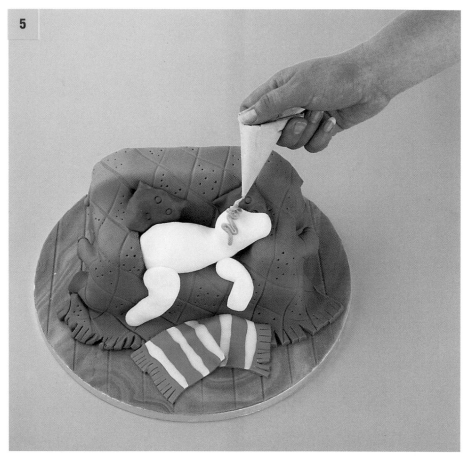

5

3

7 To make the dog, first roll 150 g (5 oz) white sugarpaste into a skittle shape for his body(4). You don't have to be too precise with this shape as it will be covered with royal icing. Press a nose into one end and lay on the sofa.
   Make two 10 g (¼ oz) white sugarpaste sausage shapes for the front and back legs and stick into position.

(Again, don't tie yourself in knots trying to make anatomically correct limbs as the long hair will hide any problems.)

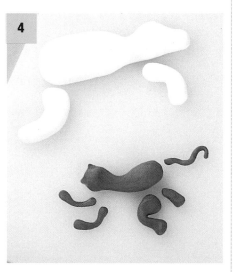

4

8 Fill one piping bag with white royal icing and one with grey icing. Pipe white icing haphazardly over the dog's body (5). Pipe a squiggly mass to the left of the dog's head for his left paw. Pipe the grey icing over the head area. Finish with a tiny ball of black sugarpaste for his nose and a pink sugarpaste tongue.

Carol suggests

This is such a useful cake to have in your repertoire because once you have mastered it you can sit anything on the couch, from footballers to Santa Claus!

9 For the cat, first roll 30 g (1 oz) grey sugarpaste into a sort of sausage with a bulbous end shape (4). Pinch two ears out of the head and stick into position on the back of the cake. Make two tiny sausage shapes for the front paws and two larger ones for the back legs.
   Bend and stick into position and add a longish string for his tail. Paint on the stripes and facial details with black food colour paste (see page 24 for hints about painting on sugarpaste).

Candles

Stick small balls of sugarpaste around the edges of the board as candleholders (see page 25 for details).

Computer

Ever felt like this when using a computer? I know I did a couple of times when writing this book! I think this scene of a teenager at the computer surrounded by mess is a rather familiar sight. For a nice personal touch, make the figure resemble the recipient as much as you can.

1 Begin by covering the 25 cm (10 in) cake board with its exotic green and orange spotted carpet. Dust your worksurface with icing sugar and moisten the top of the cake board with water. Roll out the green sugarpaste until it's approximately 15 cm (6 in) square. Take about 10 g (¼ oz) orange sugarpaste, break it into small pieces and roll into balls. Place these on top of the green square. Continue to roll out the icing to about a 20 cm (8 in) square, pressing the orange balls into the green sugarpaste (see photograph 4, Sleepy Puppy cake, page 51). Lift and place the icing onto the cake board and roll the icing up to and over the edges of the cake board. Trim and neaten the edges. Place the covered board to one side.

2 Form the computer desk from the thin cake board and cake. Using a ruler, pencil, scalpel and cutting board, mark and cut a 10.5 cm (4 in) square out of one corner of the cake board (1). Place the board to one side.

Level the top of the cake. Using a ruler and a sharp knife, cut a 9 cm (3½ in) square out of one corner of the cake. Slice 2.5 cm (1 in) off the small cut-out square and cut this into a rectangle shape for the seat. Cut the shape of the computer monitor out of the leftover.

3 Slice the main cake horizontally and fill with a layer of buttercream. Reassemble the cake and spread a thin covering of buttercream over the top and sides of the cake.

4 Roll and knead 300 g (10½ oz) white sugarpaste, the brown sugarpaste and 60 g (2 oz) yellow sugarpaste together to achieve a light woodgrain effect (see page 8 for instructions on how to do this). Measure the height of your cake and note down the measurement. Roll out the woodgrained sugarpaste and cut out a strip 72 cm (28 in) long and as wide as the height of your cake. Keep the leftover icing. Slide a knife under the length of the icing to loosen any sections that might have stuck to your worksurface and roll up the icing loosely like a bandage. Starting from the back, unwind and press around the sides of the cake. Trim and neaten the top edges.

Carefully lift and place the cake into position on the cake board.

5 To make the top of the desk, moisten the thin cake board with a little water. Re-roll the leftover woodgrain icing and place over the board. Roll it up to and over the edges. Trim and neaten the edges and place the covered board on top of the main cake.

Carol suggests

You may find it easier and less sticky to lift the cake using a long fish slice.

6 Spread buttercream over the top and sides of the sponge computer and seat. Cover the seat with 75 g (2½ oz) black sugarpaste.

Place the seat into position in front of the desk. You will not need to stick it to the board it will be held in place when the figure is positioned.

INGREDIENTS
- Icing sugar for rolling out
- 250 g (8 oz) green sugarpaste
- 15 g (½ oz) orange sugarpaste
- 18 cm (10 in) square sponge cake
- 1 quantity buttercream (see page 17)
- 475 g (1 lb 1 oz) white sugarpaste
- 60 g (2 oz) brown sugarpaste
- 75 g (2½ oz) yellow sugarpaste
- 90 g (3 oz) black sugarpaste
- 300 g (10½ oz) mid-grey sugarpaste
- Assorted food colour pastes, including black
- 120 g (4 oz) pale blue sugarpaste
- 45 g (1½ oz) flesh-coloured sugarpaste
- 30 g (1 oz) light grey sugarpaste
- 30 g (1 oz) red sugarpaste

EQUIPMENT
- 25 cm (10 in) square cake board
- Rolling pin
- Small sharp knife
- 23 cm (9 in) thin square cake board
- Ruler
- Pencil
- Scalpel
- Cutting board
- Carving knife
- Palette knife
- Fish slice (optional)
- Paintbrush
- Piping nozzle (any)
- Piping bag (see page 24)

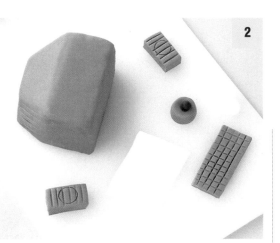

2

7 Roll out and cover the computer with 200 g (7 oz) mid-grey sugarpaste. Press a few lines into the back of it with the back of a knife. Roll out about 30 g (1 oz) mid-grey sugarpaste and cut out a small rectangle for the keyboard. Press lines both ways across the rectangle to resemble the keys (2).

To make the computer screen, thinly roll out about 15 g (½ oz) white sugarpaste and cut out a rectangle. Stick onto the front of the computer and paint an image onto the screen using food colours (see page 24 for hints about painting on sugarpaste).

8 To make the speakers, cut two thick rectangles out of 45 g (1½ oz) mid-grey sugarpaste. Press lines horizontally across each speaker with the back of a knife and a circle using something small and round such as a piping nozzle or drinking straw (2).

To make the joystick, roll about 10 g (¼ oz) mid-grey sugarpaste into a thick disc. Stick a small curved black sugarpaste sausage on the top for the handle. Roll a tiny bit of white sugarpaste into a mouse shape and press a couple of lines into the end. Arrange and stick the computer and accessories in position on the desk. The wires connecting all of the pieces will be added later, so leave space on the desk for these.

Carol suggests

If the image on the screen looks too complicated, settle for painting or sticking sugarpaste numbers on for the child's age.

9 To make the figure, roll 75 g (2½ oz) pale blue sugarpaste into a sausage, about 23 cm (9 in) long (3). Bend it into a horseshoe shape and stick onto the seat so that the right leg dangles down the front and the left leg is bent to the side slightly. Mould 15 g (½ oz) white sugarpaste into an oval for his trainer. Bend it into a banana shape and stick on the end of the left leg so that the toe rests on the floor.

10 Roll 75 g (2½ oz) white sugarpaste into a conical shape for the figure's body. Pinch lightly around the base to form a thickish frill and stick in position on top of the trousers. The figure should lean forwards onto the desk. Roll 30 g (1 oz) flesh-coloured sugarpaste into a ball and stick on top of the body. Poke a hole into the lower part of the face with the end of a paintbrush. Pull the brush downwards slightly to leave an anguished mouth shape. Stick a small ball of sugarpaste just above for a nose.

11 Roll 30 g (1 oz) white sugarpaste into a sausage and cut in half for the arms. Bend both arms at the elbow and stick into position. Divide 5 g (⅛ oz) flesh-coloured sugarpaste in half and roll into two balls for the hands. Flatten both hands and stick in position; one clasping the joystick, the other over his forehead.

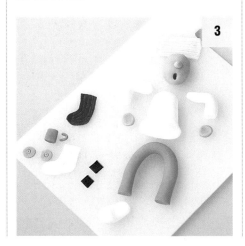

3

12 To make the hair, roll out 10 g (¼ oz) yellow sugarpaste and cut out a strip. Press lines down its length with the back of a knife, then stick over the top of the head. Paint a few lines on the trainers with black food colour paste.

13 Cut little squares out of leftover sugarpaste for disc cases and use the piping nozzle to make a circular indent in the middle of the square. Scatter around the desk and floor. Small squares of black sugarpaste can be cut to look like floppy disks and placed about the cake. To make the CD's, roll out the light grey sugarpaste and cut out discs using a piping nozzle. Poke a hole in the centre of each one and again scatter around the scene. Place a little black-coloured buttercream or royal icing into a piping bag and pipe a mass of wiggly wires over the top of the desk and floor around and behind the computer.

14 Make the plates and sandwiches out of 30 g (1 oz) pale blue sugarpaste and 10 g (¼ oz) red and white sugarpaste (see the Birthday Picnic cake on page 86 for instructions). To make the mugs, roll 10 g (¼ oz) pale blue sugarpaste into a sausage. Cut four pieces and stick a tiny curved sugarpaste string on the side of each for handles.

15 For the socks, roll out about 10 g (¼ oz) both red and white sugar-paste. Cut out some rounded "L" shapes. Press lines down their length and drape around the floor and desk. Fill any remaining gaps around the scene with scrunched-up scraps of sugarpaste to look like discarded clothing.

Candles

Stick candles into small balls of sugarpaste and place around the floor and desk. Ensure that none are underneath the edge of the desk.

Sleeping Teddy

A bed cake is a classic design and worth learning to master as once you can make your bed, you can literally lie anything in it! Read pages 21–24 on making figures and faces and place the cake's recipient in the bed. You could also personalize the "teddy bear" and the family pet at the foot of the bed for the birthday boy or girl.

Read pages 21–24

1

1 Level the top of the cake and turn upside down. Slice horizontally and fill the middle of the cake with buttercream. Reassemble the cake and place slightly towards the rear of the cake board. Spread a thin layer of buttercream around the top and sides of the cake and keep the leftover. Wipe away any crumbs, then dust your worksurface with icing sugar and knead about 600 g (1 lb 5 oz) white sugarpaste until pliable. Roll it out and place over the top of the cake. Smooth it into position and trim away any excess from the base of the cake.

2 Take about 150 g (5 oz) white sugarpaste and 60 g (2 oz) dark brown. Roll the two together to give a woodgrain effect (see page 8). Moisten the exposed cake board with a little water. Roll out the sugarpaste and cover the board in four sections (see page 20). Press a few lines into the icing using a ruler to give the effect of floorboards. To make the nails, press a few circles into the icing using the end of a drinking straw.

3 Make the teddy's pillow by shaping about 120 g (4 oz) white sugarpaste into a rectangle. Press the end of a paintbrush around the edges of the pillow to form a frill (1), and stick it into position on the bed using a little water.

4 To make the teddy, take 100 g (3½ oz) golden brown coloured sugarpaste and mould it into a thick disc shape (1). Stick two small balls of brown sugarpaste onto the teddy's head for his ears. Poke a small hollow into each one using the end of a paintbrush. Roll about 10 g (¼ oz) blue sugarpaste into a triangle for his nightcap and stick onto his head. Add a tiny ball of white for a pom-pom. Roll another 10 g (¼ oz) white sugarpaste into an oval for the bear's muzzle and stick onto his face. Poke a mouth shape into the muzzle using a paintbrush and paint a nose and two eyes onto the bear using black food colour. Stick the head onto the pillow.

INGREDIENTS

- 18 cm (7 in) square sponge cake (see page 12)
- 1 quantity buttercream (see page 17)
- Icing sugar for rolling out
- 1600 g (3 lb 8 oz) white sugarpaste
- 160 g (5 ½ oz) dark brown sugarpaste
- 150 g (5 oz) golden brown sugarpaste
- Black, blue, green and red food colour pastes
- 60 g (2 oz) blue sugarpaste
- 15 g (½ oz) flesh-coloured sugarpaste
- 30 g (1 oz) red sugarpaste
- 12–14 chocolate finger biscuits or similar

EQUIPMENT

- Carving knife
- Palette knife
- Rolling pin
- Small sharp knife
- 30 cm (12 in) square cake board
- Ruler or straight edge
- Drinking straw
- Paintbrush

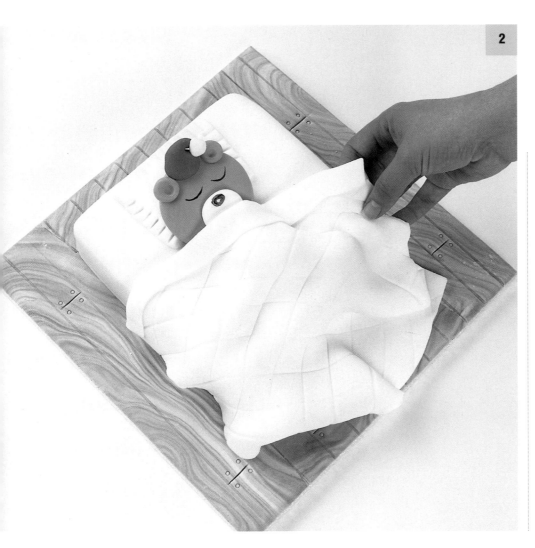

6 To make the arms, roll two 10 g (¼ oz) lumps of blue icing into carrot shapes and stick them so that they protrude out from under the blankets. Roll 10 g (¼ oz) flesh-coloured icing into a ball for the doll's head (3).

Paint on eyes, mouth and cheeks with food colour and add tiny balls of sugarpaste for his ears and nose and a fringed strip for his hair. Stick onto one of the bear's arms. Roll two 10 g (¼ oz) lumps of golden brown icing into flattened discs for the bear's paws and stick onto the arms. Bend one of them around the doll's head as though he is cuddling it.

Paint a pattern if you wish onto the quilt and some stripes onto the exposed bottom sheet (see page 24 for tips about painting on sugarpaste).

Stick a line of chocolate finger or wafer biscuits along the top edge of the bed to form the headboard. Use leftover buttercream as glue!

5 Stick one 60 g (2 oz) lump and two 15 g (½ oz) lumps of sugarpaste onto the bed in the bear's tummy and feet positions. Moisten these lumps with a little water. To make the coverings, roll about 200 g (7 oz) white sugarpaste into a strip about 38 cm (15 in) long. Slice a little off one long edge to neaten. Roll out a further 350 g (12½ oz) white sugarpaste to the same length. Using the edge of a ruler, press diagonal lines into the icing one way, then the other. Moisten the thinner strip with water. Place the larger strip on top so that it just overlaps. Bend the smaller strip back over the quilted strip so that it looks like a sheet, then neaten the edges and place the coverings on top of the bear (2).

Carol suggests

Use the blankets to hide any problem areas you may have lurking on the cake beneath!

Decorating Variation

This simplified version shows that the design works just as well using a round cake instead of a square shape. Also, on this cake, the quilt is made out of one solid colour. Not only will this save you some time, but it might also calm your nerves if painting on sugarpaste makes you jittery!

Carol suggests

Have the hands on the clock pointing towards the recipient's age, if they're under 12 that is!

7 To make the cupboard, pull a little dark brown sugarpaste off a 100 g (3 ½ oz) lump, and put to one side. Roll and shape the rest into a rectangle (3). Use the remaining brown sugarpaste to make a small flat rectangle to stick on top of the cupboard and a tiny ball shape for the handle.

Paint or stick a black rectangle on the front of the cupboard and use black food colour paste to paint an outline for the cupboard door.

For the clock, roll about 10 g (¼ oz) red sugarpaste into a thick disc. Stick a flat disc of white on the front and add a tiny flat red ball to the top. Use black food colour paste to paint dots for numbers and two arrows for the hands.

8 To make the slippers, roll three 10 g (¼ oz) lumps of blue sugarpaste into flattish oval shapes. Cut one in half. Stick one of the halves on top of one of the whole oval shapes, letting it stick up from the base of the slipper a little (you could do this by placing the end of a paintbrush underneath the half-oval). Add a bit of texture by poking it a few times with the end of a paintbrush. Repeat for the other slipper.

9 For the rug, thinly roll out 15 g (½ oz) red sugarpaste. Cut it into a rectangle. Press lines into it with the back of a knife and cut a tiny fringe.

10 For the cat, roll about 30 g (1 oz) white sugarpaste into a sausage shape. Pinch ears into one end and bend the sausage round into virtually a circle. Add a tail and paint on the features and pattern.

Candles

Place your candles into sugarpaste discs or balls around the side of the cake, well away from the actual cake.

Jungle Explorer

Using the sides of the cake to provide cunning, under-cover support, our intrepid explorer treks his way through perilous icing rainforest, unaware that his every move is being watched by eager party animals! If you plan to use candles on this cake, read the candle note before starting.

1 Level the top of the cake so that it sits securely when placed upside-down in the centre of the cake board. Slice the centre of the cake and fill with buttercream, then spread a layer of buttercream around the sides and top. Roll out 450 g (1 lb) black sugarpaste and use to cover the cake. Don't worry about any cracks – imperfections will be hidden by the trees. Moisten the board with a little water and cover with 100 g (3½ oz) orange sugarpaste (use the bandage technique shown on page 20).

2 To make the tree trunks, thinly roll out about 120 g (4 oz) dark brown sugarpaste and cut out as many 10 x 2 cm (4 x ½ in) strips as possible.

1

Press a few horizontal lines into each one with the back of a knife and stick them all around the side of the cake (1). Scrunch and re-roll the icing as necessary.

3 To make the explorer, begin with two 10 g (¼ oz) light brown "lozenge" shapes for his feet. Stick these against the side of the cake with the front foot pointing upwards and the back foot bent with the toes on the floor. Divide 5 g (⅛ oz) white sugarpaste in two and roll each half into a thick disc shape for his socks (2). Press a couple of horizontal lines around each sock with the back of a knife. Stick the socks onto the shoes.

2

4 Roll and cut 5 g (⅛ oz) flesh-coloured sugarpaste into two sausages for his legs. Also roll and cut out two small khaki squares for his shorts. Stick the front leg against the cake and stick one of the khaki squares over the top. Stick the second leg overlapping the khaki square and cover with the second khaki square.

5 Make his jacket out of 10 g (¼ oz) khaki sugarpaste. Mould it into a flat, conical shape and stick it in place over the top of his shorts. Press a line down the front of the jacket and add buttons by using the end of a drinking straw. Squash a 5 g (⅛ oz) ball of flesh-coloured sugarpaste into a thick disc for his head and stick onto the torso. Poke a small hollow for his mouth.

6 Cut out a small red rectangle for his rucksack and stick behind his back (and against the cake).

To make his arms, roll 5 g (⅛ oz) khaki-coloured sugarpaste into a sausage and cut in half. Flatten each arm slightly; bend at the elbow and stick into position on the cake.

Cut out a thin string of red sugarpaste and stick around the front of his left arm to look like the strap of the rucksack.

INGREDIENTS

▸ 1 pudding bowl cake (see page 13)
▸ ½ quantity buttercream (see page 17)
▸ Icing sugar for rolling out
▸ 500 g (1 lb 2 oz) black sugarpaste
▸ 200 g (7 oz) orange sugarpaste
▸ 120 g (4 oz) dark brown sugarpaste
▸ 60 g (2 oz) light brown sugarpaste
▸ 30 g (1 oz) white sugarpaste
▸ 30 g (1 oz) flesh-coloured sugarpaste*
▸ 30 g (1 oz) khaki-coloured sugarpaste*
▸ 15 g (½ oz) red sugarpaste
▸ 15 g (½ oz) cream sugarpaste
▸ 15 g (½ oz) yellow sugarpaste
▸ 100 g (3½ oz) grey sugarpaste
▸ 5 g (⅛ oz) pink sugarpaste
▸ 200 g (7 oz) light green sugarpaste
▸ 200 g (7 oz) dark green sugarpaste
▸ Black and dark brown food colour pastes

*Note: To make flesh-coloured sugarpaste, use "paprika" food colour paste or knead a little yellow and pink sugarpaste together. To make khaki-coloured sugarpaste, either use "gooseberry" green food colour paste or mix some yellow and green sugarpaste together.

EQUIPMENT

▸ 25 cm (10 in) round cake board
▸ Carving knife
▸ Palette knife
▸ Rolling pin
▸ Small sharp knife
▸ Drinking straw
▸ Heart shaped cutter (optional)
▸ Paintbrushes

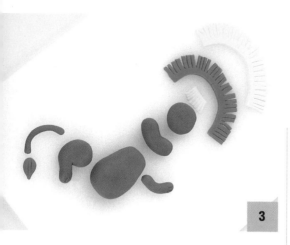

3

7 Roll up a thin strip of orange sugarpaste like a bandage and stick on top of the rucksack. Mould 10 g (¼ oz) cream sugarpaste into a semi-circle for his hat and tweak the ends into points for a brim. Stick on top of his head, covering the top half of his face, and add one flattened blob of flesh-coloured sugarpaste for his nose and two more for hands.

8 To make the lion, knead together 30 g (1 oz) light brown sugarpaste and 60 g (2 oz) orange sugarpaste to make a tan colour. Mould 30 g (1 oz) of the tan sugarpaste into a conical shape for his body (3) and stick up against the side of the cake.

Make his back leg by rolling 10 g (¼ oz) sugarpaste into a tennis racquet shape. Then bend the rounded end forwards towards the thinner end and stick on the side of the lion. Press a couple of lines into the end of the paw. Make a small sausage shape for the front paw and stick into position as though holding on to one of the trees.

9 Roll 10 g (¼ oz) tan sugarpaste into a ball for his head. Roll a further 10 g (¼ oz) into a banana shape for his muzzle and stick onto the front of his face. To make his mane, cut out two thin strips, one from yellow sugarpaste, the other from orange sugarpaste. Cut a fringe down one side of each strip. Stick the orange strip around the lion's head

Carol suggests

Use the leaves to hide any cracks or imperfections!

and the yellow one behind. Make or stick some leftover yellow fringe onto the lion's forehead.

Add a thin string of tan sugarpaste for his tail and finish off with a little orange sugarpaste tear shape. Press a couple of lines into the tail.

4

10 To make the elephant's body, roll 45 g (1 ½ oz) grey sugarpaste into a cone (4). Stick against the side of the cake. Shape 30 g (1 oz) grey sugarpaste into a tennis racquet shape to form his head and trunk, and stick onto the body. Press a few lines into the trunk. Roll 10 g (¼ oz) grey sugarpaste into an oval for his ear and press a smaller pink sugarpaste oval on top of this. Stick onto the side of his head. Add two flattened white ovals for his eyes.

11 To make the bird, roll 15 g (½ oz) black sugarpaste into a cone (4). Stick on top of the cake. Make a small black ball for his head and pinch one side to flatten it. Make two cuts into the flat section and splay and tweak the icing to form his head feathers. Stick on top of the body. Stick a small red oval on the front of his chest and two red triangles for wings. Press the edge of a drinking straw into the sugarpaste to give the bird a feathered impression. Make a small, yellow triangle shape for his beak. Press a line down the length of it and bend it into a curve. Stick onto the head. Finally, stick flat green and white ovals onto the head for the eyes.

12 Roll out the light green sugarpaste and cut out a basic leaf shape (5). Press a line down the centre and make a couple of cuts into the edges. Stick onto the cake. Repeat all over using the dark green sugarpaste as well. Bend the leaves at the top of the cake up against the sides of the bird. Cut out some heart shapes with a cutter. Press a line down the centre and make cuts in the sides. Stick these around the lower part of the cake.

13 Finally, paint the facial features on the animals with some black food colour and paint little daubs of black and brown food colour onto the explorer's jacket. Using a larger brush, paint some dark brown food colour splodges around the base of the cake to create an animal skin effect.

Candles

Make up the cake as directed but either use a bigger cake board or position the cake towards the rear of the board. This should give you room to place some icing rocks as candleholders at the front.

5

Christmas

This particular cake works well with any of the luscious fruit cake recipes on pages 14–15. It's also a winner with the vanilla and chocolate recipes too. It must be Christmas!

It using a fruit cake:

1 Place the cake onto the cake board and carve a few little dips and hollows into it to form a slightly irregular shape. Drizzle the brandy or rum over the top of the cake, if you wish, and spread the boiled apricot jam over the top and sides.

Knead the marzipan until pliable then roll out and lay over the top of the cake. Starting from the top of the cake, to prevent air from getting trapped there, smooth the marzipan into position. Trim and neaten the marzipan around the base, then brush the marzipan and exposed cake board with boiled water.

Carol suggests

An easy way to soften marzipan is to microwave it unwrapped on high for about 15 seconds.

If using a sponge cake:

1 Carve the cake into a slightly irregular shape, then slice in half horizontally. Fill with a layer of buttercream, then reassemble the cake. Place in the centre of the cake board and spread a thin covering of buttercream over the top and sides of the cake.

Brush the exposed cake board around the base of the cake with a little water to lightly moisten it.

1

For all cakes:

2 Knead and roll out 700 g (1 lb 9 oz) white sugarpaste, then lift and place over both the cake and board. Starting from the centre, smooth the icing into position. Try to cover the entire board as well as the cake. Don't worry if you have any gaps or cracks. Do the best you can and cover any problem areas or cracks with "snowballs" of white sugarpaste later. Trim and neaten the edges.

3 To make the trees, knead 30 g (1 oz) black sugarpaste and 100 g (3½ oz) green together to make a dark green colour. Divide the sugarpaste into five pieces and roll each into a carrot shape.

Holding one "carrot" gently at the base, start snipping little "V" shapes from the top down with a clean pair of scissors (1). Stick the tree onto the cake with a little water. Don't worry if the base squashes out of shape slightly as this can be hidden by snow later. Tweak the top into a neat point.

Repeat for the other four trees.

Carol suggests

For extra security you can insert a strand of raw dried spaghetti through the body and head of the characters if you wish.

INGREDIENTS

If using a fruit cake:
- 20 cm (8 in) round fruit cake (see pages 14–15)
- 2 tbsp brandy or rum (optional)
- 3 tbsp apricot jam
- 600 g (1 lb 4 oz) marzipan

If using a sponge cake:
- 20 cm (8 in) round sponge cake (see page 12)
- 1 quantity buttercream (see page 17)

For all cakes:
- Icing sugar for rolling out
- 800 g (1 lb 12 oz) white sugarpaste
- 100 g (3½ oz) black sugarpaste
- 125 g (4 oz) green sugarpaste
- 100 g (3½ oz) red sugarpaste
- 60 g (2 oz) flesh-coloured sugarpaste
- 100 g (3½ oz) brown sugarpaste
- Black and blue food colour pastes
- 10 g (¼ oz) orange sugarpaste
- 3 tbsp white royal icing (optional) (see page 18)
- 3 strands raw, dried spaghetti (optional)

EQUIPMENT
- Rolling pin
- Small sharp knife
- 25 cm (10 in) round cake board
- Carving knife
- Small, clean scissors
- Paintbrush
- Piping bag (optional)

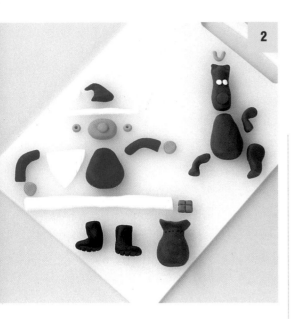

4 To make Santa, first shape 45 g (1½ oz) red sugarpaste into a conical shape for his body (2). Stick into position towards the front of the cake. Roll 10 g (¼ oz) flesh-coloured sugarpaste into a ball and stick onto his head. Roll about 5 g (⅛ oz) red sugarpaste into a triangle for his hat. Tweak the end over and stick on his head.

5 To make his boots, roll 20 g (¾ oz) black sugarpaste into a sausage about 12 cm (5 in) long. Cut the sausage in half and bend one end of each half to form two "L" shapes. Stick the boots just in front of his body, as if in a sitting position. Press a few horizontal lines into the sole of each boot using the back of a knife.

6 Roll 30 g (1 oz) white sugarpaste into a sausage about 15 cm (6 in) long. Starting from his back, lay and stick the sausage around his body and over his boots for the trim on his coat. Press a few hollows into the trim using the end of a paintbrush. Make a beard by thinly rolling out 10 g (¼ oz) white sugarpaste. Press lines down its length and stick it around the lower part of Santa's face.

Roll the leftover icing into a small sausage and ball. Stick the sausage around the base of the hat and the ball on the end of the point. Add two flesh-coloured balls for ears and one for a nose. Poke a few holes into the white hat trimmings and one into either ear with the end of a paintbrush.

7 To make the sack, roll 30 g (1 oz) brown sugarpaste into a conical shape. With the widest part of the cone forming the base of the sack, carefully pinch around the other end to form the neck of the sack (2). Cut out a small green sugarpaste square for the parcel and press a cross into it with the back of a knife. Stick the parcel into the top of the sack and scrunch the neck of the sack around it. Stick the sack in position between Santa's legs. Using the tip of a sharp knife, press a line of small stitches around the neck of the sack.

8 To make Rudolph, first roll 30 g (1 oz) brown sugarpaste into a cone for his body (2). Stick this onto the cake so that it leans against Santa. Roll 10 g (¼ oz) brown sugarpaste into a sausage shape for his head. Pinch two ears out of one end and stick onto the body.

Make two tiny sausage shapes for his arm and the foot closest to Santa. Slightly flatten one end of each sausage to form a hoof shape and stick them into position. His foot should drape over Santa's boot. For the other larger leg, roll 15 g (½ oz) into a sausage. Squash and flatten one end slightly to form a thigh and flatten the other end to make a hoof shape. Stick onto the body.

9 Stick two white flattened dots of white sugarpaste onto Rudolph's head for his eyes and a tiny curved sausage of flesh-coloured sugarpaste for his horns. Add a small ball of red for his nose and paint black food colour pupils and eyebrows on his face.

10 Make Santa's arms by rolling 15 g (½ oz) red sugarpaste into a sausage about 10 cm (4 in) long. Cut the sausage in half and stick one arm from his body to the sack and the other from his back and around Rudolph. Finally divide and roll 5 g (⅛ oz) flesh-coloured sugarpaste into two balls. Flatten each ball slightly and stick one on the end of each arm to form his hands.

11 To make the elves, first roll a 15 g (½ oz) green cone (3) and stick towards the left-hand side of the cake. Divide 10 g (¼ oz) flesh-coloured sugarpaste into two pieces and roll into ball shapes for their heads. Stick one onto the green body and the other on the ground to the right of Santa. Top both heads with a tiny green Santa hat and a nose and two ears made exactly as you did for Santa. Stick two flattened discs of flesh-coloured sugarpaste for hands in front of the elf to the left of Santa.

12 Make the naughty troll by rolling 15 g (½ oz) white sugarpaste into a cone shape (3). Roll 10 g (¼ oz) flesh-coloured sugarpaste into a ball for his head and stick onto the body. Stick a small triangle of red sugarpaste onto his head for his hat, but don't add the trimmings! Paint two "S" shapes for his eyebrows and two dots for his eyes with black food colour paste. Then stick two pointed pieces of flesh-coloured sugarpaste, one on each side of his head, for his ears and another ball on the front of his face for his nose. Finally add a sneaky, smiley mouth and stick him into position peeking through the fir trees at the rear of the cake.

13 For the lying down penguin, roll 15 g (½ oz) black sugarpaste into a sausage shape (3). Cut two pointed wings out of the sides with the scissors and lay the bird flat on the cake. Roll and flatten two small orange sugarpaste ball shapes for his feet and make a pointy triangular shape for his beak. Stick into position. Make a red Santa hat for his head.

14 For the sitting-up penguin, roll 15 g (½ oz) black sugarpaste into a cone and snip out two wing shapes. Stick a disc of white sugarpaste onto his tummy and add feet, a beak and a hat.

15 Stick a few white sugarpaste "snowballs" around the cake. Place about two tablespoons of white royal icing into a piping bag. Pipe a squiggly line around the base of the trees and the characters. Using a damp paintbrush, stroke and pull the icing to look like snowdrifts (4). Rinse and

reuse the brush as necessary. Paint a little watery blue food colour around the cake, to bring out the snow.

When this is dry, sift a little icing sugar over the top of the scene to look like freshly fallen snow.

Candles

If you should want to incorporate candles into this scene, stick them into snow balls on the cake or board.

Caterpillar

This is such an easy cake to put together. If you haven't time to bake fairy cakes, cheat and use packs of shop-bought cakes instead. If it's the thought of all that piped buttercream that worries you, then sandwich the cakes together with "splodges" instead!

1 Lay all your cakes roughly in position on the board to check whether there are enough and also to work out the colours. Note that the "head" cake stands on top of another cake to give it added height.

2 If using a piping nozzle , cut a small triangle off the pointed end of the piping bag (see page 24) and insert the nozzle. Place a couple of tablespoons of buttercream into the bag and fold the end over twice to close it. If you're not using a nozzle, place the buttercream into the bag, close it and then snip a triangle off the end. Starting from the centre of the fairy cakes, pipe a spiral on top of each cake (1). If you find this too tricky, just spoon a dollop of butter-cream on the top of the cake instead!

3 Stick the cakes in position around the board as soon as you've buttercreamed them (2). If you leave them too long, the buttercream will start to dry out and lose its sticking ability.

4 To make the caterpillar's face, begin with the eyes. Use about 5 g (⅛ oz) white sugarpaste. Pull off a tiny bit and put to one side. Divide the rest in half and roll into two balls. Squash the two balls to form two flat discs and press on to the caterpillar's head.

Keep a small piece of the black sugarpaste to one side, then make two smaller black sugarpaste discs in the same way for the pupils and roll the reserved white sugarpaste into two dots for the highlights.

5 From the rest of the black sugarpaste, make a small button for his nose and a short sausage shape for his mouth. Stick into position on the face.

6 To make each foot, roll about 15 g (½ oz) white sugarpaste into an oval. It will get a little busy in the middle of the cake if you allow two feet per cake so limit it to just five or six in the centre. Stick each foot as required onto the board with a little water.

7 Cut a short length (about 8 cm/3 in) of liquorice bootlace for each foot. Using the end of a paintbrush, poke a hole in a foot and a hole in the top of the corresponding cake, then insert the liquorice leg (3). Work around the cake.

8 Finally insert two lollipops into the caterpillar's head for his feelers and spoon the green-coloured dessicated coconut around the board.

Carol suggests

If you can't get hold of liquorice bootlaces or anything similar you could substitute chocolate sticks or sections of raw, dried spaghetti instead. Alternatively use lollipops, upside down without the sugarpaste feet.

INGREDIENTS

▶ About 14 coloured fairy cakes (see page 13)
▶ 1 quantity buttercream (see page 17)
▶ 350 g (12 oz) white sugarpaste
▶ 15 g (½ oz) black sugarpaste
▶ 3 thin liquorice bootlaces or similar (colour of your choice)
▶ 2 lollipops
▶ 45 g (1½ oz) green-coloured desiccated coconut (see page 18)

EQUIPMENT

▶ 30 cm (12 in) round cake board
▶ Piping bag (optional)
▶ Star piping nozzle (optional)
▶ Scissors
▶ Paintbrush

Racing Car

I have a suspicion that this cake might appeal just as much to boys (and girls) of forty as those of four! If you don't have a loaf tin in which to bake your cake simply cut a square one to size instead.

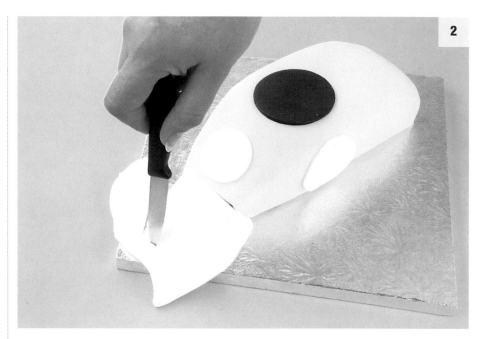

1 Carve a tapering slope into the front of the cake. Round and neaten the top edges. Place into position diagonally across the cake board. Roll 30 g (1 oz) white sugarpaste into a pointed carrot shape and lay in front of the cake (1). Slice the cake horizontally and fill with a layer of buttercream. Reassemble then spread a thin layer of buttercream over the top and sides.

2 Dust your worksurface with icing sugar and knead 450 g (1 lb) yellow sugarpaste until soft and pliable. Roll it out and place over the car. Smooth the icing over the top and down the sides. If it starts to fall into pleats, lift and gently pull and fan the icing out. Slice about 3 cm (1 in) yellow sugarpaste off the point of the car to reveal the white sugarpaste "carrot" beneath. Moisten the "carrot" with a little water and keep the discarded yellow sugarpaste. Trim and neaten around the base.

3 Roll out 30 g (1 oz) black sugarpaste and cut out a round, flat disc. Stick this on top of the car. Clean your fingers and roll out 30 g (1 oz) white sugarpaste. Using a circle cutter or a lid, cut out three discs. Stick one on the bonnet of the car and the other two on the sides. Knead the leftover white sugarpaste plus an additional 30 g (1 oz) together and roll out to the same thickness as the yellow sugarpaste that you used to cover the car. Slice a little off one edge and lay over the pointed front of the car (2). Butt the edge of the white right up against the edge of the yellow to make a neat seam and trim around the edges.

4 Roll 250 g (9 oz) white sugarpaste into a ball shape for the helmet. Stick this on the top black disc. Pull off and keep 20 g (¾ oz) red sugarpaste. Roll the rest into a thick, flattish conical shape and stick this behind the driver's head. Cut a thick rectangle out of 60 g (2 oz) black sugarpaste and stick this behind the red sugarpaste. Roll out 30 g (1 oz) yellow sugarpaste and cut out a slightly larger but thinner rectangle. Stick this on top of the black.

INGREDIENTS

- Cake baked in a 500 g (2lb) loaf tin (see page 13)
- 350 g (12 oz) white sugarpaste
- 1 quantity buttercream (see page 17)
- Icing sugar for rolling out
- 500 g (1 lb 2 oz) yellow sugarpaste
- 450 g (1 lb) black sugarpaste
- 150 g (5 oz) red sugarpaste
- 300 g (10½ oz) green sugarpaste
- 15 g (½ oz) flesh-coloured sugarpaste
- Black food colour paste
- 1 sheet rice paper
- 15 g (½ oz) green-coloured dessicated coconut (optional, see page 18)

EQUIPMENT

- Carving knife
- 25 cm (10 in) square cake board
- Palette knife
- Rolling pin
- Cake smoothers (optional)
- Small sharp knife
- Circle cutters or various sized lids
- Paintbrush
- Template for smoke (see page 94)
- Non-toxic pencil
- Scissors

5 Moisten the cake board around the car with a little water. Knead and thinly roll out 300 g (10 oz) green sugarpaste. Lay the sugarpaste in sections around the base of the cake (see page 20) until the board is hidden. Smooth into position, then trim and neaten the edges.

Carol suggests

You could always leave the board plain or cover it with green-coloured dessicated coconut completely if you prefer.

6 Make four thick 90 g (3 oz) black sugarpaste discs for the wheels and stick them into position around the car. Thinly roll out 30 g (1 oz) yellow sugarpaste and cut out four discs. Stick one in the centre of each wheel. Finish each one with a small flattened ball of red sugarpaste.

7 Roll out 5 g (⅛ oz) flesh-coloured sugarpaste and cut out a rectangle for the driver's face, seen through the helmet visor. Cut a tiny triangle off each corner to make a long, flat oval shape then stick it onto the front of the helmet, allowing it to curve slightly.

Paint the eyes on the flesh-coloured sugarpaste and the numbers on the car with black food colour. (See page 24 for hints about painting on sugarpaste.)

Carol suggests

You could match the number of the car to the age of the recipient.

8 To make the tortoise, begin with the shell. Partially knead 30 g (1 oz) white sugarpaste and 5 g (⅛ oz) leftover green sugarpaste together to achieve a green marbled effect. Roll it into a ball, then pinch along the base to form a shell shape (3). Place to one side.

9 Roll 10 g (¼ oz) black sugarpaste into a sausage and cut in half for the wheels. Stand them side by side and stick the shell on top.

Decorate the wheels with tiny discs of white and red sugarpaste to match the racing car behind.

3

10 Stick a small ball of white sugarpaste on the front of the shell for his helmet and decorate with a very small flesh-coloured rectangle. Paint eyes on this and a few squares on the shell with the black food colour paste. Stick the tortoise on the board.

11 Draw a line of "smoke" (see template on page 94) on a piece of rice paper and cut it out. Stick the "smoke" behind the tortoise, supporting it with balls of sugarpaste. To finish, you could sprinkle a few strands of coloured dessicated coconut around the board.

Candles

Make some "pebble" candle holders as shown on page 25 and stick these around the board keeping well away from the rice paper.

Gingerbread

This cake is so easy to make. Once the gingerbread figures are baked, everyone can have a go at decorating them. If there's not enough room on the cake for them all, serve them individually as teatime biscuit treats!

1 Mix up and bake the gingerbread characters (see page 16 for recipe and details) and make at least two house shapes just in case one goes wrong or accidentally gets eaten! When they're cool, decorate the gingerbread people as you wish. You could cut out sugarpaste clothes in a range of colours and stick them on with a little water.

Use buttercream to pipe squiggly hair or to "glue" on small sweets or cake decorations. You could even paint expressions with food colour. Let your creativity shine through (1). When finished, place to one side.

2 To tile the roof of the house, you will need both the pale and dark blue sugarpastes. Roll both shades out thinly and cut out discs using either a circle

Carol suggests

If you look in the "Home Baking" section at the supermarket, you should be able to find packs of "writing icing". These are small tubes of ready-to-use colours and are ideal for use on projects such as this.

cutter or a small lid. Scrunch and re-roll the leftover icing as necessary. Stick a line of discs along the bottom of the roof using a little water. Place a second line above them so that they overlap slightly (2). Continue right to the top, then trim any tiles as necessary.

Add sugarpaste rectangles and squares for the doors and windows and any other home decorating embellishments that take your fancy! When finished, place to one side.

INGREDIENTS

- Gingerbread characters (see page 16)
- 2 gingerbread house shapes (minimum)
- 30 g (1 oz) red sugarpaste
- 30 g (1 oz) green sugarpaste
- 1 quantity buttercream (see page 17)
- Small sweets, silver balls, icing, cake decorations etc for decorating gingerbread
- 30 g (1 oz) pale blue sugarpaste
- 30 g (1 oz) dark blue sugarpaste
- 20 cm (8 in) square sponge cake
- 1500 g (3 lb 6 oz) white sugarpaste
- 4 tbsp white royal icing (see page 18)

EQUIPMENT

- Gingerbread men/women cutters
- Templates for house shape (see page 94)
- Piping bags (see page 24)
- Scissors
- Star nozzle (optional)
- Paintbrush
- Rolling pin
- Circle cutter or lid
- Small sharp knife
- Carving knife
- 25 cm (10 in) square cake board

Decorating Variations

Here are Jemma, Belinda and Natalie's decorated gingerbreads. As you can see, the scope for creativity is endless and you can never be too young to decorate gingerbread!

If you're pushed for time, or simply prefer a more traditional approach, you could choose the more conventional raisin and glacé cherry attire!

3 To prepare the cake itself, begin by carving it into a slightly irregular shape by cutting out a few shallow dips and hollows. Slice the cake in half horizontally and fill with buttercream. Reassemble the cake and place in position on the cake board, slightly towards the rear. Spread a thin layer of buttercream over the top and sides of the cake and dab a little water onto the exposed cake board around the base of the cake.

4 Knead 900 g (2 lb) white sugarpaste until pliable. Roll it out to a width of about 33 cm (13 in) and lift and lay over the cake and board.
   Starting from the middle of the cake, smooth and press the icing carefully into position. Trim and neaten the edges around the board, and reserve any offcuts from around the board for use later.

Carol suggests

Don't worry about any cracks or bits of exposed cake board as these can be hidden by icing "boulders" later!

5 To provide hidden support for the house, place a lump of about 90 g (3 oz) white sugarpaste in a rectangular shape towards the back of the cake. Pipe

Carol suggests

If you make your gingerbread more than a day in advance, or if there's a lot of humidity or moisture in the air (common in kitchens), you may find that your gingerbread has softened and gone a bit "bendy". If so, place on a baking tray and re-bake undecorated on a low heat for 5-10 minutes.

a line of royal icing along the front and carefully stand the house in position (3). Make sure it stands securely. If it starts to lean forwards, place a few white icing "boulders" in front of it.

3

6 Place about a tablespoon of white royal icing into a piping bag, preferably fitted with a star nozzle, and pipe either a "snail trail" or a line of dots around the outside of the house (see page 25 for notes on piping).
   If you don't possess a star nozzle, place the royal icing directly into the bag and snip a tiny triangle off the end.

7 Make a path from the front door by sticking about seven blue sugarpaste discs in a wavy line towards the front of the cake. Stick the two smaller characters in front of the house. Keep them standing upright with the aid of a large sugarpaste "boulder" and a dab of royal icing. Stick the two largest characters at the front against the side of the actual cake itself.

8 Finally, fill any gaps or cover any marks on the white sugarpaste with icing "boulders". Stick small sweets over and around the cake with royal icing for extra decoration.

Candles

Insert your candles into the white sugarpaste "boulders" around the cake. Add more as necessary, ensuring all are kept well away from the gingerbread.

Wicked Witch

An ugly green-faced witch and her big bubbling cauldron full of jelly snakes, eyeballs, spiders and other revolting things. What could be more horrible than that?

1 This is one of those rare occasions where if your cake rose enthusiastically in the oven it is actually a good thing. To make the cake into a cauldron shape, carve away any cracked, crusty bits (but try to retain a fairly rounded look). It is up to you which way you use the cake. Look at it both upside-down and the right way up to see which way looks the most cauldron-like.

If your pudding bowl cake came out of the oven looking pretty flat and level on top, it is probably best to use it upside-down with the widest part forming the base.

2 Slice the cake twice horizontally and fill the layers with buttercream. Reassemble the cake and position towards the rear of the cake board. Spread a thin covering of buttercream over the outside of the cake.

3 Dust your worksurface with icing sugar and knead 500 g (1lb 2 oz) black sugarpaste until pliable. Roll out and place over the cake. Smooth it into position. You should be able to lift and gently pull and fan out any sections that are tending to fall into pleats. If you have problems with awkward folds or cracks, just smooth out as best as you can and remember to cover with "flames" later.

4 Trim and keep the excess black icing from around the base. Out of this, roll 90 g (3 oz) into a long sausage. Paint a ring of water on top of the cake and lay the sausage in a circle to form the neck of the cauldron.

5 Make a handle by rolling 15 g (½ oz) grey sugarpaste into a thinnish string. Stick this onto the front of the cauldron, in a curve. Roll two 5 g (⅛ oz) balls of grey sugarpaste into balls and squash them both into discs. Press a circle into each one with a lid or piping nozzle, and a small hollow in the centre with the end of a paintbrush. Stick one on either end of the handle.

Carol suggests

Don't worry about icing sugar marks on the black icing at this stage, these will be dealt with at the end.

6 Thinly roll out 90 g (3 oz) yellow sugarpaste for the flames. Holding your knife almost vertical and just using the tip, cut out a very simple leaf shape. You can use the templates or cut these basic shapes freehand. Cut out as many as you can and stick around the base of the cauldron (1). Re-roll the icing as necessary.

7 To make the witch, first roll 30 g (1 oz) purple sugarpaste into a flattish conical shape to form the top of her body (2). Stick this onto the back of the cauldron, so that it rests on the bowl and uses the neck of the cauldron for support. For extra security, insert a couple of strands of raw, dried spaghetti through the body into the cake below.

INGREDIENTS

- 1 pudding bowl cake (see page 13)
- 1 quantity buttercream (see page 17)
- Icing sugar for rolling out
- 1500 g (3 lb 6 oz) black sugarpaste
- 30 g (1 oz) grey sugarpaste
- 90 g (3 oz) yellow sugarpaste
- 45 g (1½ oz) purple sugarpaste
- 2 strands raw, dried spaghetti
- 45 g (1½ oz) green sugarpaste
- 45 g (1½ oz) white sugarpaste
- Black, red, orange and green food colour pastes
- 1 breadstick
- 90 g (3 oz) blue sugarpaste
- 5 g (⅛ oz) red sugarpaste
- 2 tbsp royal icing (optional) (see page 18)
- 10 chocolate flakes or finger biscuits
- 1 green-coloured fairy cake
- 30 g (1 oz) desiccated coconut

EQUIPMENT

- Carving knife
- Palette knife
- 25 cm (10 in) round cake board
- Small sharp knife
- Lid or piping nozzle
- Paintbrush
- Templates for flames and cloak (see page 94)
- Drinking straw
- Pastry brush

8 For her head, roll 30 g (1 oz) green sugarpaste into an upside-down tear shape. Stick this onto the body so that her chin (the thinnest part) rests on her chest. Check that it all sits securely.

Squeeze two tiny balls of white sugarpaste into "lemon" shapes, then squash and flatten to make her eyes. Stick onto her face. Make her eyebrows by rolling two tiny bits of green sugarpaste into little strings then bending them into "S" shapes. Stick one over each eye.

Add a tiny bent triangle of green icing for her nose and two either side of her head for her ears. Paint in the pupils with black food colour and add a mouth and a few dots for her whiskers!

9 To make the hair, roll out a tiny piece of leftover yellow sugarpaste and press a few lines down its length with the back of a knife. Cut out two long tapering triangles and stick one on either side of her head.

For the hat, roll about 5 g (⅛ oz) black sugarpaste into a cone. Tweak the tip into a wonky point and stick on top of her head. Roll a tiny piece of black sugarpaste into a sausage and stick around the base of the hat for a brim.

10 To make the arms, roll 5 g (⅛ oz) purple sugarpaste into a sausage and cut in half. Bend each of the halves slightly to form an elbow and stick into position against the body resting the wrists on the neck of the cauldron.

Place a 9 cm (3¼ in) section of breadstick into position. "Hold" it in place with two hands made from flattened green sugarpaste balls stuck at the ends of the arms and over the breadstick.

11 To make the cloak, roll out 90 g (3 oz) black sugarpaste. Cut out a tapering rectangle, using the template on page 94 if necessary. Stick the cloak around the back of the witch allowing the top edge to frame the face slightly to form a collar.

12 Make two eyeballs by rolling two 15 g (½ oz) lumps of white sugarpaste into balls and placing into the top of the cauldron (3). Paint two black pupils onto of the eyes and a few red ghoulish blood vessels.

Also, while you have the red food colour paste out, paint a red centre in the middle of each flame around the side of the cauldron.

13 To make the snake, use the blue sugarpaste and 10 g (¼ oz) black sugarpaste. Partially roll the two colours together to make a sort of blackish-blue woodgrain effect (see page 8). Roll the icing into a sausage, leaving one end slightly thicker than the other to form a head, and make a small cut into the base of the head for his mouth.

Arrange, drape and stick the snake down the side of the cauldron and onto the board. Stick two tiny white balls on top of his head for his eyes and paint two black food colour dots for the pupils. Make a tiny string of red sugarpaste for his tongue, sticking it from his mouth onto the board. Make a small cut and splay the end of the tongue.

Using a drinking straw held at an angle, press tiny "U" shapes all over the snake to give the impression of scales.

14 Brush away any icing sugar smudges around the sides of the cauldron with a large, damp (not soaking wet) brush such as a pastry brush. If it looks very shiny, leave to dry before putting the drips of "boiling liquid" down the sides of the cake or they will begin to dissolve.

15 To make the "boiling liquid" in the top of the cauldron, either water down a couple of tablespoons of royal icing to a spoonable consistency or mix 15 ml (2 tbsp) of water into 120 g (4 oz) icing sugar (add more sugar or water as necessary).

Stir in some orange food colour paste to the liquid and carefully spoon the icing into the top of the cauldron (4). Add a few artistic dribbles down the sides.

Carol suggests

If you don't want to make a green spider, hunt around your local sweet shop for jelly insects or snake sweets instead.

16 Arrange sections of chocolate flakes or biscuits around the base of cauldron to look like logs. You can "glue" them in place with a little buttercream if you wish. Place a green spider cake in front of the cauldron (see the Horrible Bug cake on page 40 for instructions on how to make this).

Take 30 g (1 oz) desiccated coconut and colour it green (see page 18) Spoon the "grass" around the base of the cake.

Candles

You should have enough room at the front of the board to position some sugarpaste "pebble" candle holders well away from the main cake. See page 25 for instructions about how to make them.

Birthday Picnic

Here's a birthday picnic that looks good enough to eat! For an added personal touch, try to make the child look as much like the recipient as possible. The little elephant model would also work equally as well on a leaving cake with the caption "We'll never forget you!"

2

1 Begin by covering the board with the green sugarpaste, using the "all-in-one" method shown on page 19 and place to one side. Level the top of the cake and turn it upside-down so that you have a nice, flat surface on the top. Slice horizontally and fill the centre with buttercream. Spread a liberal layer of buttercream around the sides of the cake and a thin layer over the top. Using a fish slice, to stop your fingers getting sticky, lift and place the cake in the centre of the covered board.

2 To make the tablecloth, first measure the height of your cake and double the number. Add this figure to the diameter across the top of the cake (in my case, this came to 35 cm/14 in). You will now need either a round plate or cake board with a diameter the same

1

as this new measurement (if you have neither, cut out a paper or card template instead). Roll out 600 g (1 lb 5 oz) white sugarpaste. Place your template on top and cut round it using the tip of a sharp knife. Carefully lift up the sugarpaste disc, (wiggle a long palette knife under it to loosen it if it sticks) and place on top of the cake. Allow the sides to fall into neat pleats and folds, tweaking them where necessary (1). Place the covered cake to one side.

INGREDIENTS

▶ 20 cm (8 in) round cake
▶ 1 quantity buttercream (see page 17)
▶ Icing sugar for rolling out
▶ 300 g (10 oz) green sugarpaste
▶ 700 g (1lb 9 oz) white sugarpaste
▶ 100 g (3½ oz) pale blue sugarpaste
▶ 15 g (½ oz) red sugarpaste
▶ 90 g (3 oz) dark brown sugarpaste
▶ 15 g (½ oz) light brown sugarpaste
▶ 120 g (4 oz) grey sugarpaste
▶ 4 strands raw, dried spaghetti
▶ 30 g (1 oz) black sugarpaste
▶ 60 g (2 oz) dark pink sugarpaste
▶ 30 g (1 oz) yellow sugarpaste
▶ 30 g (1 oz) flesh-coloured sugarpaste
▶ 75 g (2½ oz) pale pink sugarpaste
▶ Red food colour paste

3 For the crockery, use a set of circle cutters, icing nozzles or small lids from foodstuffs as cutters. Roll out 30 g (1 oz) pale blue sugarpaste and cut out one disc about 5 cm (2 in) wide, four disks with a 4 cm (1½ in) diameter and four disks, about 2.5 cm (1 in) wide. Re-roll the icing as necessary. The plates can be left plain or you could paint on a coloured pattern and press a slightly smaller cutter or lid just inside each disc to leave a circular imprint (2).

EQUIPMENT

▶ 30 cm (12 in) round cake board
▶ Rolling pin
▶ Fish slice (optional)
▶ Ruler or tape measure
▶ 35 cm (14 in) cake board or plate (see step 2)
▶ Small, sharp knife
▶ Palette knife
▶ Assorted circle cutters or lids
▶ Birthday cake candle
▶ Large drinking straw
▶ Cocktail stick
▶ Paintbrush
▶ Piping nozzle (any size)
▶ Five petal flower cutter (optional)

4 To make the birthday cake, roll 30 g (1 oz) white sugarpaste into a thick disc. Using the end of a paintbrush, poke and drag a series of dents around the base of the disc. Turn the disc upside-down and repeat.

Stick the cake onto the largest plate and eight tiny red sugarpaste balls around the top, for glacé cherries (2). Stick a small ball of white sugarpaste in the centre and stick a candle on the top. Place to one side.

5 For the sandwiches, take 10 g (¼ oz) white sugarpaste and 5 g (⅛ oz) red sugarpaste. Divide the white sugarpaste in half and roll all three pieces of sugarpaste into thin strips and stick on top of each other with the red in the centre. Cut into a rectangle then into squares. Divide each square into quarters diagonally (2).

Arrange and stick about five sandwiches onto one of the larger plates with water. Place another couple of sandwiches on two of the smaller plates. Take a "bite" out of one sandwich using the end of a drinking straw and place this, the plate and any leftover sandwiches to one side.

6 To make the iced buns, roll 5 g (⅛ oz) dark brown sugarpaste into eight ball shapes, then flatten each one to make a disc. Top each bun with a smaller flattened disc of white sugarpaste and a minute ball of red sugarpaste to look like a cherry.

Stick seven buns onto a serving plate and one onto a small plate. Place to one side.

7 For the shortbread, roll out 10 g (¼ oz) light brown sugarpaste and cut into a rectangle. Divide into about ten smaller rectangles and, using the point on a cocktail stick, poke six tiny holes into the top of each biscuit. Pile the shortbread biscuits up on a serving plate and place to one side.

8 To make the iced donuts, divide 10 g (¼ oz) light brown sugarpaste into eight pieces. Roll each piece into an oval and partially slice through each oval lengthways. Fill the centre of each donut by lying a very thin string of red and white sugarpaste down the length of the bun. Again, place to the side to decorate the cake with later.

9 To make a teapot, use 30 g (1 oz) pale blue sugarpaste. Pull off a little for the handle and spout and roll the rest into a ball. Using a piping nozzle or something similar, press a little circle into the top of the ball. Roll a little of the leftover icing into a tiny ball and stick on top of the teapot. Divide the rest in two and roll into two thin sausage shapes. Stick one on the front of the pot, bending the tip forward to look like a spout. Bend the other into a semi-circle for its handle and stick on the back and place to one side.

10 For the elephant's body, roll 60 g (2 oz) grey sugarpaste into a cone and insert a couple of short lengths of spaghetti in the top. Make two thick grey 5 g (⅛ oz) discs for his feet and stick these onto his tummy (3). Using a large (or jumbo – very apt) drinking straw, press four semi-circles into the top of each foot to look like his toes. Roll 30 g (1 oz) grey sugarpaste into a tapering sausage shape for his head and flatten the thicker end slightly. It should now look a bit like a tennis racquet. Stick the head onto the body. Press a few lines into the trunk with the back of a knife and a couple of nostrils with the end of a paintbrush.

11 To make his eyes, stick two white and two smaller black sugarpaste discs onto his face. Make another disk from grey sugarpaste and cut it in half. Stick one half over each eye. For his ears, roll 10 g (¼ oz) grey sugarpaste into a ball then flatten slightly. Repeat using a smaller dark pink sugarpaste ball. Place the pink shape on top of the grey and squash the two together. Cut the disc in half and stick one ear on either side of his head. Make a tiny yellow sugarpaste square for his napkin. Roll 5 g (⅛ oz) grey sugarpaste into two sausage shapes for his arms. Fold the napkin over the end of one of the arms and stick onto the body. Stick the other arm in place. Place to one side.

12 To make the boy figure (see page 21 for a girl figure), roll 30 g (1 oz) white sugarpaste into a cone for his body (4). For his legs, roll 30 g (1 oz) blue sugarpaste into a sausage, cut in half and stick in place. Stick a yellow sugarpaste serviette onto his front and insert a short length of dried spaghetti into his body. Roll 15 g (½ oz) flesh-coloured sugarpaste into a ball for his head and stick onto the body. Poke a round mouth and add two tiny white and black sugarpaste discs for his eyes and a small flesh-coloured nose.

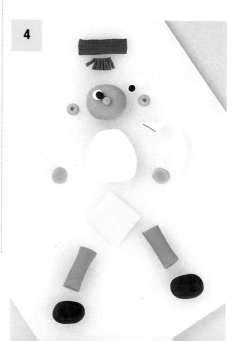

7

13 The boy's hair is made by rolling and cutting out a small dark brown sugarpaste rectangle. Press lines down its length with the back of a knife and lay the strip over the top of the boy's head. Cut out tiny rectangles and make small cuts along one of its longer sides to make a fringe. Roll a little flesh-coloured sugarpaste into two tiny balls for his ears and stick onto the side of his head. Poke a little hollow into both with the end of a paintbrush.

14 Divide and roll about 10 g (¼ oz) white sugarpaste into two small sausage shapes for his arms. Bend both at the elbow and stick onto the body. Stick the sandwich, with a bite taken out of it, onto his chest between the arms and, using two tiny flattened discs of flesh-coloured sugarpaste as hands, position these as though holding the sandwich. Finally, make two 5 g (⅛ oz) black sugarpaste ovals for feet.

15 Place the boy, elephant, cake, teapot and plates (except for one small one) on top of the cake. "Glue" them in place with a little water. To make the teddy, roll 30 g (1 oz) pale pink sugarpaste into a cone (5). Stick on the front edge of the cake. Insert a length of spaghetti into the body. Divide 15 g (½ oz) pink sugarpaste in half and roll into two sausage shapes for his legs. Bend the ends up to form feet

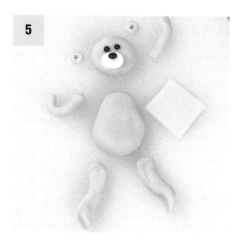

and stick onto the body so that they dangle over the edge of the cake. Make a yellow sugarpaste serviette and a 15 g (½ oz) pink sugarpaste ball for his head and stick both into place. Add a small white icing oval for his muzzle and tiny black sugarpaste eyes and nose. Stick these slightly off-centre as though he's looking downwards. Stick two pink sugarpaste balls on his head for his ears and make a hole in each with the end of a paintbrush. Make two small pink sugarpaste sausages for his arms and stick into place.

6

16 To make the chimp, roll 30 g (1 oz) dark brown sugarpaste into a cone and stick on the board, using the cake for support. Pull one third off a 15 g (½ oz) lump of dark brown sugarpaste and form an oval for his back foot (6). Stick into position bending the top of the foot forwards slightly. Mould

the remaining icing into a tennis racquet shape. Bend the end up to make a foot and stick onto the side of the monkey. Roll about 15 g (½ oz) dark brown icing into a ball for his head and stick in place.

17 Flatten a small banana-shaped piece of flesh-coloured icing and stick onto the face for his muzzle. Press something curved such as the edge of a lid or cutter into the muzzle to make a mouth. Add white discs and black icing dots for eyes and a tiny flesh-coloured dot for a nose. Finally, roll about 5 g (⅛ oz) brown sugarpaste into two long, thin sausages for his arms. Stick one as though reaching up to the table and the other around one of the spare sandwiches. Stick the remaining plate of food on the ground by his side.

18 For the flowers to decorate the cake, roll out about 50 g (1¾ oz) pink sugarpaste and cut out about eight flowers using the petal cutter (see page 25 in Basic Techniques section for instructions). Finally, paint red food colour stripes onto the tablecloth (7).

Candles

If you only need a few candles, make the miniature cake larger and stand them in that. Alternatively place the candles into icing rocks around the board (see page 25). Keep well away from the sides of the cake.

Cookie Monster

The only really frightening thing about this particular monster is the number of calories he contains! It's a good thing birthdays only come around once a year!

1 Begin by making the monster's head. Take one of the pudding bowl cakes and, using a carving knife, slice away enough cake from the widest part at the bottom so that it sits securely without wobbling.

For the face, roll out 100 g (3½ oz) cream-coloured sugarpaste and cut out a rough circle about 10 cm (4 in) in diameter (1). Stick this onto the front of the cake using either a little buttercream, jam or melted chocolate. Wipe away any surplus that oozes out from under the face when in place.

2 Take three 5 g (⅛ oz) lumps of green sugarpaste. Roll each one into a ball, then flatten slightly. Stick two in position as eyes and one as a nose, using a little water (taking care not to use too much or they'll just slide off). Poke two hollows for nostrils in the nose with the end of a paintbrush.

3 Break off a little black sugarpaste and roll into two small balls. Flatten both balls and stick onto the monster's eyes. Roll the rest of the black sugarpaste out flat and cut out a curved mouth shape. Stick this onto the face. Roll the red sugarpaste into a tapering sausage shape for the monster's tongue. Squash slightly and stick onto the monster's mouth.

4 To finish the eyes, flatten two tiny balls of cream-coloured sugarpaste and stick onto the pupils. Roll and flatten a 20 g (¾ oz) ball of cream sugarpaste and cut in half. Stick the two halves over the top of the eyes to form eyelids.

Using a little black food colour and a fine paint brush, paint a couple of lines under each eye, one line under the mouth and a curve at each corner of the mouth (see page 24 for hints about painting on sugarpaste). Place this cake to one side for the moment.

5 Make sure the second cake will sit on its base nice and securely as this will form the monster's body. If its top is very domed, slice a little off it to make it flat enough to support the head. Place the body cake into position in the middle of the cake board. Melt the white chocolate (see chocolate cake recipe page 13 for instructions about how to do this). When it has all melted, pour onto the cake board around the cake (if the bowl is very hot, you may need to hold it using oven gloves or a tea-towel). Using a spatula or palette knife, spread out the melted chocolate to cover the whole board.

6 In a second bowl, melt the dark chocolate. Pour it over the top of the base cake (2). Spread the chocolate over and down the sides of the cake using the palette knife and allow it to run into and mingle with the white chocolate on the cake board. Place the head into position on top of the body.

INGREDIENTS

- 2 chocolate chip pudding bowl cakes
- ¼ quantity buttercream (see page 17)
- 150 g (5 oz) cream sugarpaste
- 15 g (⅜ oz) green sugarpaste
- 15 g (⅜ oz) black sugarpaste
- 5 g (⅛ oz) red sugarpaste
- Black food colour paste
- 200 g (7 oz) white chocolate
- 200 g (7 oz) dark chocolate
- 1 packet chocolate and nut biscuits
- 4 mini chocolate rolls
- White and milk chocolate buttons
- 200 g (7 oz) milk chocolate

EQUIPMENT

- Carving knife
- Rolling pin
- Small sharp knife
- Paintbrush
- Palette knife
- 30 cm (12 in) round cake board
- Spatula
- Plastic cake dowel (optional)
- Piping bag (see page 24)
- Scissors

7 Press a ring of about ten chocolate and nut biscuits around the base of the monster's body. Cut a small triangle off the ends of four mini chocolate rolls and stick them into position as the monster's arms and legs. Stick two cookies on the ends of his legs as feet and a line of white chocolate buttons down the front of his tummy. Scatter white and milk chocolate buttons around the cake board.

8 Melt the milk chocolate and pour over the monster's head, taking care to work around the face. Make sure the

Carol suggests

Although the chocolate itself should be enough to hold the head in place on top of the base cake, if you're at all nervous, you can stick a plastic cake dowel into the body and slot the head onto it. (see the Doll cake on page 55 for details.)

Decorating Variation

This version was made using a single tier. Again the board was coated with white chocolate and the body with milk chocolate. Biscuits were stuck around the base of the cake and the board. The simple face was made out of white sugarpaste and white chocolate buttons but you could easily substitute marshmallows or small, coloured sweets if you prefer. The whole confection was then drizzled with both milk and white chocolate.

head is completely covered and allow it to drip freely onto the board and cookies below. Cut or break a cookie in half and stick onto his head for his ears. After about five minutes (depending on the temperature of your kitchen), when the chocolate on the head has cooled slightly, you can "rough it up" to give the monster's head a little texture. To do this, press the flat edge of a palette knife gently onto the chocolate, then pull it away to leave a little peak.

9 To finish, use a spatula to scrape out the remaining milk chocolate left in the bowl and place into a piping bag (see page 24). Fold over the ends to close it and snip a tiny triangle off the end. Pipe the chocolate over the top of the cake and the covered board (3).

Candles

Make balls of cream- or brown-coloured sugarpaste candle holders and stick around the edges of the board keeping them well away from the cake itself.

Templates

PRINCESS CAKE page 46
template actual size

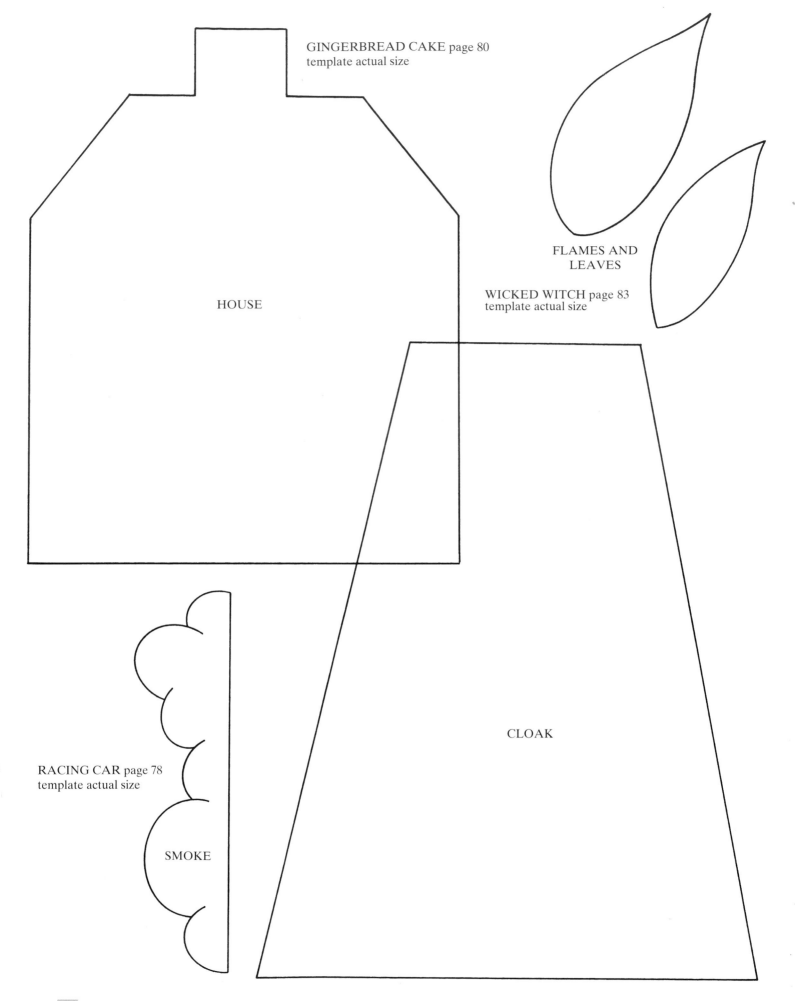

GINGERBREAD CAKE page 80
template actual size

FLAMES AND
LEAVES

WICKED WITCH page 83
template actual size

HOUSE

CLOAK

RACING CAR page 78
template actual size

SMOKE

Suppliers

These are just a few of the specialist cake shops dotted around the country. Most offer mail order services but if you prefer to shop in person and none are convenient then look in your local phone book or call Culpitt's Customer Service line on 01670 842800 to find your nearest supplier.

PIPE DREAMS
2 Bell Lane
Eton Wick
Berkshire
Tel: 01753 865682

TORBAY CAKE CRAFT
5 Seaway Road
Paignton
Devon TQ3 2NX
Tel: 01803 550178

THE CAKE MAKER'S DEPOT
57 The Tything
Worcester WR1 1TJ
Tel: 01905 25468

CREATIVE CAKES & SUPPLIES
379 Clarkston Road
Cathcart
Glasgow G44 3JG
Tel: 0141 633 0392

CORTEIL & BARRATT
40 High Street
Ewell Village
Epsom
Surrey KT17 1RW
Tel: 020 8393 0032
Fax: 020 8786 8779
http://www.city2000.com/sh/cakecraft.html

CONFECTIONERY SUPPLIES
29–31 Lower Cathedral Road
Cardiff CF1 8LU
Tel: 01222 372161
(Outlets also in Bristol, Hereford & Swansea)

LINDEN CAKE GALLERY
15 Cross Street
Wakefield WF1 3BW
Tel: 01924 299449

LONDON SUGARART CENTRE
12 Selkirk Road
London SW17
Tel: 020 8767 8558
Fax: 020 8767 9939

SQUIRES KITCHEN SUGARCRAFT
Alfred House
Hones Business Park
Farnham, Surrey GU8 8BB
Tel: 01252 727572
Fax: 01252 714714
www.squires-group.co.uk

RETAIL OUTLETS:
CULPITT LTD
Jubilee Industrial Estate
Ashington NE63 8UQ
Tel: 01670 814545
Fax 0800 801235
http://www.culpitt.com
Customer service & enquiry line: 01670 842800

GUY, PAUL & CO. LTD
Unit B4, Foundry Way
Little End Road
Eaton Socon
Cambs. PE19 3TR
Tel: 01480 472545 / 472645
Fax: 01480 405608

RENSHAW SCOTT LTD
Crown Street
Liverpool L8 7RF
Tel: 0151 706 8282
Fax: 0151 706 8201

Clyde Street
Carluke ML8 5BD
Tel: 01555 770711
Fax: 01555 772237
Customer service line:
0151 706 8282
www.renshawscott.com

SOUTH AFRICA
SOUTH BAKELS
55 Section Street
Paarden Eiland 7420
Cape Town
Tel: (021) 511 1381

EDCO MARKETING
Pogson Street
Sydenham
Port Elizabeth 6001
Tel: (041) 451 2613

CATERING MANAGEMENT SERVICES CC
Unit 14-15
9 Mahogany Field Way
Springfield Park 4034
Durban
Tel: (031) 579 1910

QUALITY DISTRIBUTORS (PTY) LTD
52 Tannery Road
Hamilton
Bloemfontein 9301
Tel: (051) 435 7224

SOUTHERN ARTS & CRAFTS
Flat no. 5
JD Viljoen Building
105 Main Street
Rosettenville 2130
Johannesburg
Tel: (011) 683 6566

AUSTRALIA
THE CAKE DECORATING CENTRE
15 Adelaide Arcade
Adelaide
South Australia 5000
Tel: (08) 8223 1719

HOLLYWOOD CAKE DECORATIONS
52 Beach Street
Kogarah
New South Wales 2217
Tel: (02) 9587 1533

CAKE AND ICING CENTRE
651 Samford Road
Michelton
Queensland 4053
Tel: (07) 3355 3443

PETERSEN'S CAKE DECORATIONS
Rear 698 Beaufort Street
Mt Lawley
West Australia 6050
Tel: (08) 9271 1692

NEW ZEALAND
THE CAKE BOX
Shop 4, 59 Juliet Ave
Howick
Auckland
Tel: (09) 537 4212

GOLDING HANDCRAFTS
Harbour City Centre
Lambton Quay
Wellington
Tel: (04) 472 4496

ICING SPECIALISTS EQUIPMENT
Shop 6, Church Corner Mall
Riccarton
Christchurch
Tel: (03) 348 6828

SPECIAL OCCASIONS
2 Catherine Place
Henderson
Auckland
Tel: (09) 838 9881

SPOTLIGHT
19 Link Drive
Glenfield
Auckland
Tel: (09) 444 0220
Also stores in Hamilton, New Plymouth, Wellington and Christchurch

Index

Entries in bold indicate projects

a

air bubbles under sugarpaste 11
all-in-one method 19
animals, making from sugarpaste 23-24

b

Baby Dinosaur 38
basic equipment 26
basic recipes 12-18
basic techniques 19-21, 23-25
Birthday Picnic 86, 88-89
buttercream 17

c

cake:
  square 19
  round 19
cake board:
  all-in-one covering 19
  bandage covering 20
  edging with ribbons 21
  covering 19-20
candle holders 25
candles 25
Caterpillar 76
Cheeky Pets 60, 62
chocolate
  cake, microwaved 16
  chocolate chip cake 13
  fruit cake 15
  sponge cake 13
  truffles 17
Christmas 73-75
colouring
  desiccated coconut 18
  sugar granules 18
  sugarpaste 7
Computer 63, 64
Cookie Monster 90, 92
covering a cake 19
cracks in sugarpaste 11
cutting sugarpaste 10

d

desiccated coconut:
  as grass 18
  as gravel 18
  colouring 18
Doll, Rag 55-57

f

faces, making from sugarpaste 21
fairy cakes 13
Fairy Town 36-37
figures:
  making from sugarpaste 21
  supporting 21
Fishing Pond 52, 54
Football Team 43-44
fruit cake 14
  chocolate 15
  traditional 14
  tropical 15

g

gingerbread 16
Gingerbread 80, 82
glace icing 18
grass, from desiccated coconut 18
gravel, from desiccated coconut 18

h

Horrible Bug 40, 42

i

icing:
  glace 18
  recipes 17-18
  royal 18
  sugar marks 11

j

Jungle Explorer 70, 72

l

loaf tin, cakes made in 13

m

Madeira sponge cake 12
making a piping bag 24
marble effect 8
microwave cakes 16
modelling sugarpaste 21
multi-coloured effect 8

p

painting on sugarpaste 24
  bleeding colours 6, 24

piping bag:
  making 24
  techniques 24
plasterer technique 11
Princess 46, 48-49
pudding bowl, cakes made in 13

r

Racing Car 78-79
Rag Doll 55-57
ribbon edging on boards 21
royal icing 18

s

Sketchbook 33, 34
Sleeping Teddy 66, 68-69
Sleepy Puppy 50-51
Space Age 30, 32
special effects 8
square cakes 19
sugar, colouring 18
sugarpaste 6-11
  air bubbles 11
  colouring 7
  covering cakes 19
  cracks in 11
  cutting 10
  making animals 23-24
  making faces 21
  making figures 21
  marble effect 8
  modelling 21
  multi-coloured effect 8
  painting on 24
  recipe 17
  sticking together 9
  storing models 10
  using 6
  watermarks 11
  woodgrain effect 8

t

templates 93-94
tropical fruit cake 15
troubleshooting 11
truffles, chocolate 17

u v w

Upside Down 58-58
vanilla cake, microwaved 16
watermarks, sugarpaste 11
Wicked Witch 83-84
woodgrain effect 8